MW01094103

DO IT FOR YOUR

SELFIE!

A GUIDE TO LOVING YOURSELF, REDESIGNING YOUR LIFE, AND GETTING ALIGNED FROM WITHIN

DENISE MARSH

Copyright © 2022 by Denise Marsh

All rights reserved. No part of this publication may be reproduced, distributed, or transmitted in any form or by any means, including photocopying, recording, or other electronic or mechanical methods, without the prior written permission of the author/publisher, except in the case of brief quotations embodied in critical reviews and certain other noncommercial uses permitted by copyright law.

For permission requests, write to the author at: www.denisemarsh.net

Do It For Your SELFIE! / Denise Marsh—1st ed.

Paperback ISBN 978-1-956989-07-6
Hardcover ISBN 978-1-956989-02-1

DEDICATION

To my younger self, I can't go back and give you a hug to let you know we turned out OK, but I can and did write a book about it.

To my daughter, Dona-Car'n, A.K.A. my wombmate! You have taught me more than any book or class ever could. I love you more than cheese fries!

To my husband Tim, just thinking about you makes me smile. Your support and patience have been a huge part of my healing and I love you for it.

To my mother, I love that we continue to choose to love and get to truly know one another. So glad we answer each other's calls now. HAHAHA.

To my brothers Darius and Chaun, you aren't with me physically, but I have felt you both every single day on this journey. P.S. Why did both of you leave me to deal with Ma alone?

CONTENTS

Praise for DO IT FOR YOUR SELFIE!

If you've ever struggled to love yourself, this book will hit you – hard! But you're in good hands: Denise exudes warmth and encouragement, and she'll have you feeling like self-love is totally doable in no time. Eye-opening, heartwarming, and empowering, this book isn't one you quickly skim. It's one you take your time with...and do it for your selfie!

Tracie Kendziora, author, book coach, and editor

Denise gets raw and real in her book Do It For Your SELFIE!, showing us that even if we've been through hard things, we still deserve happiness. Denise doesn't just tell you, she shows you by sharing stories of incredible women who overcame obstacles but eventually found their path to self-love. It will inspire you to love your SELFIE once and for all.

Lindsey Smith, author of *Eat Your Feeling*s

Incredible. Inspiring. Life-changing. Denise shares the true secret to transforming your life from the inside out. Even if you've hit rock bottom, this book will help you get a new lease on life.

Noelle Bloom, founder of *Joy Today*

Wow! From the moment I picked up this book I did not want to put it down. I took my time between chapters and was truly able to absorb the stories of the women highlighted here. By doing so my definition of self love and self image have shifted and grown more than I could have imagined! Denise's writing style allowed me to connect with each story while reflecting on my own journey. I can confidently say that I am a stronger person than I was before reading. Now it's your turn to be empowered, grateful, and to love your SELFIE!!

Rachel Saylor Brown, VP of Mortgage Lending, Clearwater, FL

INTRODUCTION

It took a while for me to narrow down the title, because how could I cram all of what this book is about into a few words? Then I realized the title is giving you the super short and sweet summary of what you're about to get into. I chose *Do It for Your SELFIE! A Guide to Loving Yourself, Redesigning Your Life, and Getting Aligned from Within* as the title because it actually summarizes this book in a cool way. Redesign and Align from Within is the business I am the founder and owner of. "SELFIES" represents the chapters and stories you are going to experience in this book, such as self-worth, self-image, and self-satisfaction, just to name a few. (If you haven't noticed yet, I love a play on words!) And this is definitely more of a guide than your typical self-help book. It's also like an inexpensive coaching session with me, so WIN-WIN! This book has many levels to it, and I want to encourage you to read this when you are free of distractions. You will definitely need a pen, because this book has some activities to help you out along the way. I also want to take this opportunity to say THANK YOU for choosing this book, receiving this book if it was a gift, and even reading this far into the book. Fingers crossed you keep reading until the end!

QUICK SUMMARY

Imagine someone you love deeply and completely. A child, parent, friend, or even a pet.

You love this person (or pet) with your whole heart. You want them to have the very best things in life. You want to protect this beautiful creature from harm. You want to uplift them when they're feeling down. You forgive them when they make a mistake. You encourage them to go after their goals. You celebrate their victories, big and small. You speak kindly to them, saying things like, "You're so strong." "You're so smart." "You can figure this out." "You got this."

Now, imagine taking all the love that you give so generously to someone else and giving that same love to yourself. That is what "self-love" means, and that's what this book is all about.

In this book, you'll learn:

What self-love actually means, and why it's really a collection of choices that you make every day.

Why so many women struggle with self-love, and the cost of not addressing this issue.

Specific things you can do to love yourself more.

How to build stronger self-worth, self-confidence, and other important "inner SELFIES." (They're way more important than the kind of selfie you post online!)

How to evaluate your current position on the Self-Love Spectrum, and then re-evaluate in a few weeks to see how you're improving.

How to become a woman who genuinely, seriously loves herself.

When we better ourselves, others benefit from it. This creates healthier and more joyful households, family dynamics, friendships, work environments and your social life.

Why the statistic that "79 percent of women are suffering with general self-esteem issues" is true, and how if you're part of that 79 percent there are ways to move over to the other side (Simpson 2021). Let's change those stats!

HI, IT'S ME, DENISE, YOUR SELF-LOVE COACH.

One day on the first coaching call with a new client, she told me that she didn't know how to love herself. This wasn't the first time I had heard a client, a friend, or a family member say this. How did they get to that point of not loving themselves? Better yet, did they ever know how? Fortunately, or some may say unfortunately, I understood what she meant. I too had struggled for years with not knowing how to truly love, respect, and appreciate myself or my life.

Here's my personal journey.

I remember the night he had his hands around my throat choking the life out of me as he sat on top of me while I was flat on my back in the living room of my apartment. His grip was so tight I couldn't find any room to slip my fingers in to loosen it. While he was screaming at me, "Die, just die," over and over with a look that told me he truly meant for me to die right then and there by his hands, my daughter who wasn't even two years old yet stood not even three feet from us crying. I knew at that moment this couldn't be the ending for me, but it surely felt like it. I refused to let my daughter see her mother die like that, but how was I going to stop him? As I felt myself drifting off, someone burst through our front door and pushed him off of me. This person, who I will always refer to as my savior, grabbed me in one arm and my daughter in his other arm, and ran out the door. He put us in his car and asked me where he could take us. I was crying while trying to catch my breath, and the only words that I could say were, "I almost died, I almost died." I was finally able to tell him my aunt's address, who lived not too far from me. When he parked in front of her house, he walked me and my daughter to the front door. My aunt opened the door and looked at me—me, with only a t-shirt and underwear on, holding my daughter who was wearing a onesie and a pullup, standing in the dark—and she grabbed us both into a hug. Her hug only confirmed that I was blessed to be alive.

That was a turning point in my self-hate journey, and not so much in the upward way. That incident had me questioning everything in my life. It had me questioning who I was, why I was alive, why God would give me a child while my life was so messed up, why I couldn't control my anxiety, why depression was the only feeling that felt normal, why no-one loved me enough to save me from the hell I was living in, and why my life seemed so unfair.

I survived that night physically, but mentally and emotionally something snapped and I was not OK. How did my life turn out this way, and why couldn't I see any way out of the mess my life had become? I had a daughter who depended on me to take care of her, but I was so deep in my depression I didn't know how much longer I could go on. You would think that after a near death experience I would see the light and take charge of my life. That was not the case for me. Life actually became harder and scarier for me.

The person who almost killed me made my life a living hell for years. I'm not talking about silly threats and laughing about it later. I'm talking about stalking me, leaving voice-mail messages threatening to kill me whenever he saw me, almost running me and my daughter off the highway, beating me up in front of the police station, carving the word BITCH on the entire driver's side of my car with a sharp tool while I was visiting someone, and that was just part of it. By now you're probably asking yourself if I got the police involved. Of course I did. I had a restraining order, and clearly that didn't matter because you read the part of him beating me up in front of the police station. That was nothing compared to when he found me, dragged me into an alley in broad daylight, and kicked the crap out of me. The result of that was my mother and grandmother having to come to the hospital to see what he had done. This is only a small part of what I went through physically, and the mental, emotional, and spiritual parts of me were damaged even more.

I can remember vividly one night sitting in the bathtub while my daughter, who was a toddler at the time, was sleeping in the other room, and asking myself what the point was of living. I honestly did not see why I needed to keep living a life where I was afraid, depressed, and anxious every single day. In my mind, my daughter was better off with someone who was more stable. I truly felt like I was on the brink of a nervous breakdown, and I couldn't tell anyone what was really going on. There were times I tried to tell some of my family and friends just a snippet of what I was going through. I was either told that I was crazy, that I should pray about it, that I should call the police, that they would protect me, or that maybe it was not that bad. Are you serious? Those were not solutions. I needed real help, and I needed it now. Yes, I finally did seek help because I thought I was losing my mind, and the doctor put me on pills that made me feel like a zombie. Yes, I did pray. Yes, I called the police numerous times. No, you couldn't protect me. And YES, it really was that bad. Some of my family and friends truly wanted to help me; however, they just didn't know what to do. They would try to help in some ways, but in my mind, I knew that nothing they did would really "fix" my problems.

Who is this person that did this to me? It was a guy that I loved and who I thought loved me. In the beginning of our relationship, he treated me like I was the best blessing he had ever received in his life. He made me feel loved, appreciated, and special. Why was this a need for me? There was something missing in my life, or so I thought, and he came right at the nick of time to fill that void. He made me feel protected and wanted. You see, after my parents divorced, I did not deal with that well, and no one ever asked my brothers and I if we were OK with what happened to our parents. If they had asked, we would have told them that we were not OK at all.

My brothers and I were raised to be closer than close, and we were. We did mostly everything together, and it was rare that we weren't together, especially when we were younger. I remember our mother was quiet around us, unless she was singing while cooking, cleaning, or just moving around the house. She wasn't affectionate with us; however, she made sure we were always clean and fed. I remember our father was the most kind and patient man in the entire world, and he always had something fun planned for us. I was closer to my father than my mother, and I used to think she didn't love me. My father would pray with us every night, tell us he loved us every day, and give us hugs and kisses just because. My mother didn't do those things, so in my young mind I didn't understand how she could love me if she didn't say it or show me affection. We never saw our parents argue or mistreat one another. We only saw the opposite, and that was our parents always being sweet and playful towards each other. So, before my *eighth* grade year, when they told us they were splitting up, it was a total shock to us, and it did something to each of us. I can speak for myself when I say that I didn't recover from it until my *thirties* after lots of time with my therapist. Once we moved out of our home into a new neighborhood away from our friends and our father, life changed for us in ways we weren't expecting. Our mom started working more, and our father was in our lives but it was different because we were no longer living in the same house. There were so many changes that weren't being explained to us, and I was starting to change on the inside and the outside, and not for the better.

Once I started high school, I felt lost most of the time, and I started acting out. Was it to get attention? I don't know. I just knew I stopped caring about the consequences of my actions. Being around my two brothers were the only times I truly felt OK, because if nothing else, I knew we had each other. Well, that changed quickly once I got into big trouble during the beginning of my sophomore year. My mom decided it was best to pull me out of the high school I was attending, and because of the issues I was having at home with my mom I went to live with my grandparents. I hardly ever saw my brothers, I saw my father less, and I didn't want to see or talk to my mom because I was so angry with her. I blamed my mom for the divorce, and for everything else that seemed to be going wrong in my life. You know when you're not OK, the blame game gets stronger, and mine was aimed at my mom. I eventually moved back home the summer before my junior year, because my brother Darius was starting high school, and he wanted me to attend the same school as him. I would do anything for my brothers, so I moved back home even though things between me and my mother were not any better.

The rest of my time in high school was somewhat better outside of my home, because I got a job, I had close friends, I had a boyfriend, and on the outside everything looked good. On the inside my thoughts were dark, my moods were heavy at home unless I was doing something with my brothers, and I was never pleased with the way I looked. On my heaviest day I was ninety-five pounds during my junior and senior years. That was purposeful. I had major body image issues, which was connected to other issues in my life. I decided I was going to get my act together once I was in college, and was determined to graduate with my psychology degree in four years, then move on to earn my master's and doctorate. Even though some areas of my life were a mess, I was smart and my grades reflected that.

I attended a university on a full scholarship, and I felt life was starting to look up for me. I was living in a dorm, made friends pretty quickly, and I had my entire future planned out for me. Well, those plans took an unexpected detour. Halfway through completing my degree, and working towards my big bright future, I became pregnant. I thought the doctor had the wrong person when she told me I was pregnant. I wasn't even at the doctor's office for a pregnancy test. I was there for my annual check-up. "This can't be happening," I thought. "I have to finish school, and there is no way I am telling my religious family that I am pregnant and not married!" The thoughts that ran through my head were all over the place. "How could I be pregnant?" I thought I was being careful, but apparently if you do the act that can get you pregnant there's a chance you can get pregnant. Who knew?!

Even though I was pregnant, I was still determined to continue on with my education and not stray too far away from the plan I had for myself. This was also around the time I realized that sometimes when you make plans, something out of your control can change your plans without your permission. I became extremely sick during my pregnancy, and I could not keep attending school. I had to drop out, and that was devastating for me. "So, not only am I an unwed, young, pregnant, black woman, I am also a college drop out? Oh no, no, no! This couldn't be! I cannot be another statistic." I thought I was being punished or pranked in the biggest way. But, no, this was actually my life. I could not sit in self-pity for too long, because I had a daughter to think about who would be out of my womb and in my arms soon.

On July 17, 2000, my baby was born, Dona Car'n. I named her after my mom, Donna, and my aunt Caryn. I was in love with her before she was born, but after I saw her for the first time, I couldn't imagine loving anyone more than I loved her. She was a part of me, and I couldn't believe that she was my sweet little baby. I thought to myself, everything will be fine. I can do this! I will love her, protect her, sing to her, and make sure she always knows she can depend on me.

No one told me about postpartum depression. No one told me that you could feel like you were in a pool of mud where you were repeatedly being pulled under, while someone else was trying to yank you out, and you just wanted to float in it. That is the best way I can describe how I was feeling. I could not think straight, and I was not in my right state of mind most of the time. Somewhere along the way the postpartum depression was just depression, and then anxiety wanted to join the party a couple of years later. I told my doctor what was happening, because my anxiety attacks were extremely scary and I knew I needed professional help. The medication the doctor put me on helped, but not really. I felt like a zombie on the meds I was taking, and I just couldn't seem to get myself out of this major mental and emotional hole I was in.

The first few years of my daughter's life I was not OK. Year after year I felt as though my life was getting worse, my relationships with others were not great, I was unhealthy, and I was alone. This was also around the time I almost died by the hands of someone who once told me he loved me and prayed for someone like me. I hated my life and I hated what I had become. I felt like I was living in a constant nightmare, and I felt like the worst mother in the world because I didn't know how to get better. I loved my daughter so much, but loving myself was so far from the way I felt about myself that I couldn't feel anything but shame, fear and despair. I definitely couldn't see how I could take care of my daughter when part of me wished he would've just killed me while he had the chance.

I didn't know at the time that I had to save myself. I didn't know at the time my daughter couldn't be my only reason for living. I certainly didn't know at the time that one day I would be coaching women and hosting retreats on mindset transformation, starting a podcast, speaking at various events, and writing a book to help women on their self-love journey. How could I have known that wanting to die was what I needed to go through to want to live?

Deep breath in. 1, 2, 3, 4, 5. Deep breath out. 1, 2, 3, 4, 5. Those deep breaths are for both of us. This is the first time I've shared ALL of what you just read. Some people know parts of what I have just shared, and there are parts that have never been shared with anyone until just now. Why am I sharing this now? I am no longer afraid or embarrassed to share that part of my life. I know that there is someone reading this who may be where I was, and I want them to know that even though our stories may be similar, there is a way we get to choose the ending of that chapter. There may be someone reading this who cannot relate to me at all; however, that person may still need to know that even during the darkest or most challenging time in their life, there is still a way and a reason to push forward. The key is finding it, and that starts with you rediscovering your truest self. I will not say you need to find yourself, because you are not lost. You may have just lost your way, and sometimes that is when it may seem like the hardest time to love ourselves in the way we need it most.

How do I know? Because after going through some of the hardest years that I thought would never end, I went through the most transformative years of my existence with breakthrough after breakthrough that had me seeing myself and my life through completely new lenses. I rediscovered ME, how to truly live my life on purpose, and how to replace despair with real joy. I learned how to heal from past trauma, how to forgive others to free myself from anger, how to create healthy boundaries to protect my mental and emotional health, and how to put myself first without feeling guilty about it. Because of the life changing transformation I experienced, I wanted to make it my new mission to help other women do the same. This book is a testament to my journey, and several other women who have allowed me to be a part of their transformational experience as their coach and a part of their loving R.A.W. support team.

I must tell you that I am not going to give you a magical spell, a secret potion, or a long unrealistic list of things to do in this book to help in your self-love journey. What I am going to do is share stories from my own life and from some of the women I am proud to say were once clients of mine, and some may still be as you're reading this book. In this book I will share simple and effective tips you can start applying right now that will cause shifts in the way you see yourself and how you live your life. The question is are you willing to do it? The women in this book, including myself, have learned ways to love ourselves, truly see ourselves, and live in ways at one point we didn't believe was possible. We are real people, with real challenges, and we bleed and breathe the same way you do. So, if we can do it, so can you! You may be ready to go from self-loathing to self-like, and some of you may be ready to blow the meter off the charts with how much you are ready to embrace and love yourself. Either way, you are not alone, and you are worthy of the love and life you've been thinking about, praying for, and dreaming about!

If any of what I just shared resonated with you in any way, please keep reading.

Some years ago, I decided to bring one of my childhood dreams to life, and that was to host my very first retreat to help women learn how to put themselves first without guilt and to learn how to love themselves more. YES, this was a real dream I journaled about many times when I was a child. If you were to ask me now how I knew as a child that I wanted to help women in that way, I would answer you that an almighty force gave me the vision of what would come to pass one day, and here's the kicker... IT DID! Here's the other kicker, I had to experience a whole lot of "stuff" to get to this point. Not just experience it, but heal, overcome, and grow from all of that "stuff," so that I could be in a position to help others do the same.

This is probably where I should introduce myself, or re-introduce myself for those who may have known me in the past. My name is Denise Marsh, and I am a woman who has committed to loving myself harder each day, having fun and laughing until my belly aches daily, and enjoying as much of this one earthly life that I have. Some of the things I enjoy most: having solo dance parties whenever the mood strikes; giving my fur babies their own private concert where I sing whatever random song pops into my head; traveling and spending time with my husband; laughing with and hugging my daughter; creating memories with friends and family; reading (if I don't read every day, there is a problem); watching *The Golden Girls* (I'm a HUGE *Golden Girls* fan thanks to my Grandma Gloria); and being in or near the water, which makes my soul smile.

Professionally, I am a transformational mindset coach, and I help women learn how to put themselves first without guilt, discover new ways to love themselves on all levels, and create realistic paths to bring whatever dreams they have been sitting on to life. Over the past few years, I have started my own podcast, Getting R.A.W. with Denise; I have created two journals (a thirty-one-day journal and a three-month journal); I have been a speaker on many stages and platforms; I host transformational retreats in the U.S. and internationally; and I have personally guided hundreds of women on their self-love journey to help them live their lives on purpose and be in love with it.

I decided to write this book because I wanted to use my voice and the voice of the women in this book to share our stories to offer a ton of hope, a heap of faith, a few laughs and giggles, and a whole lot of encouragement. Let this book be your new bestie. I promise she won't tell any of your secrets, and she will never judge you.

What if this book provides the voices you have been wanting to hear to reassure you that you are not alone in your personal struggles, and that there are women out there who totally GET YOU? What if one or more of the stories shared in this book are so similar to your own personal life that you feel that I am actually writing about you? What if you can finally say, *"Yes, that's totally what I'm going through,"* and not feel judged, shamed, or as though you are not smart enough?

This book is for you if you are open to an experience in the form of a book that is straight forward, honest, and raw, because no one has time for sugar coating anymore. This book is for you if you have said or are saying that you are ready to put yourself, your wants, and your desires first without feeling guilty about it. This book is most definitely for you if you are ready to stop wasting time in your life, learn a new meaning of the word **SELFIES** and how they apply to your own life, and see a new way of being, living, and loving your raw, truest self!

By the end of this book, you will have a choice to make. During your reading journey into this book, you may have some major ***WOW! I NEVER THOUGHT ABOUT IT THAT WAY*** moments, some ***OH GOSH, THAT'S ME*** moments, or ***SOUNDS GOOD, BUT CAN I REALLY CHANGE THE WAY I FEEL ABOUT...*** moments. Let me be the one to tell you right now you are capable of doing hard things, you are lovable and loving in more ways than you realize, and your life is meant to be full of joy and pleasure. I will also be the one to tell you right now that there is a difference between *wanting* and *willing*. You may *want* to majorly increase your **SELF-WORTH,** be a pro in the positive **SELF-IMAGE** department, and even learn how to fall madly in love with yourself. The question is are you *willing* to do the work, and stop making excuses as to why you cannot? Are you also ready to open yourself up to creating new beliefs around what **SELF-LOVE** truly means to you in order to become more fulfilled, and how it is possible to be OK with **SELF-VALIDATION** and not needing the approval from others you may have been seeking out most of your life? What would change for you if you were able to have more **SELF-CONFIDENCE**, so those dreams, goals, and aspirations you have can turn into your reality? How much more joy, happiness, and carefreeness would you experience if you made a loving commitment to yourself to add **SELF-SATISFACTION** as a non-negotiable in your life? All of this is possible, and you have a choice to make. Ask yourself if you are done saying that you *want* to make some life-improving changes for yourself, and if you are finally ready to say you are *willing* to do what it takes to create some life improving changes for yourself. Or, are you going to invest your time, money, and energy into reading this book and not do a darn thing to change one or more of your personal **SELFIES,** even though you know your happiness, peace of mind, and life depend on it? The choice is yours!

You may look at the chapters in this book and think there are a few you don't need because your **SELF-CONFIDENCE** is off the charts, or you don't struggle with **SELF-VALIDATION.** I am encouraging you to go along on this journey with me and the women who are featured in this book and read every single chapter. You may be surprised at what stories, questions, or suggestions jump out and grab you by the shoulders to shake some unexpected **SELF-AWARENESS** into your consciousness. Each chapter will be a guide to support you along on your **SELF-LOVE** journey, and I am here for it. Are you?

You have one known life on this earth to live. How are you choosing to honor this gift of life and live it in the best **SELFIE** mode? No life "filters" will ever be needed again if you choose yourself! It is the most **SELF-*FUL*** thing you can do! It's time to get R.A.W.!

THE R.A.W. SELF-LOVE SPECTRUM

Self-loathing: You question how anyone could like or love you. You can't find anything to love about yourself. You either keep to yourself because you think everyone is against you, or you surround yourself with people and/or relationships with people who are also self-loathing or who treat you horribly. You may have even questioned why you are alive when you can't seem to find any happiness or peace in yourself.

Self-dislike: You may say you love yourself; however, your actions say otherwise. You stay in relationships that are not good for you. You beat yourself up about your physical appearance and/or your intellect. You feel like everyone else is more important than you are. You don't feel special, loved, or appreciated by anyone, including yourself.

Self-complacency: You don't get too excited about anything revolving yourself. You go through life seeming OK in your relationships with yourself and others, and you may be happy or comfortable with your job/career; however; you don't think very well of yourself, and it's hard for you to believe others when they see you in a highly favorable way.

Self-like: You take time to get to know the current you, and enjoy the time you do spend with yourself. You take time for true self-care, or recognize that you deserve to. You are in good relationships that you value, and where you are valued. You have friends you enjoy, and who enjoy you. You are happy with your occupation, and you take steps towards fulfilling any dreams you have for your life.

Self-love: You are past the getting-to-know-you stage, and you are digging everything about yourself. You take time for the loving and sometimes challenging work that it takes to continue being true to yourself and living your life on purpose, in peace, and with flow and fun. Not only do you love yourself, but you are also in love with the person you choose to be each and every day. You love yourself so much that everyone else's love is a bonus. Because you love, respect, and understand yourself, you are able to be more loving, respectful, and understanding with others.

I want to add here that so many women I personally know, including myself, have been on each stage of the spectrum. So, while this is not a medical book written by a famous psychologist, I will say this is a book from several different women who were at one point in their lives on a part of the Self-Love Spectrum that they didn't want to be on. These women were able to find their way to self-love by being willing to do the work, finding it within themselves, and having the right type of support to believe they could see themselves in a new way.

Having trouble seeing yourself in those definitions?
Here's another way to view the Self-Love Spectrum definitions:

Self-loathing may sound like voices in your head saying that you are not worthy enough to be loved, and that you are not special enough to live an incredible life. When in this mindset, a person will show self-destructive behaviors, may not take care of their hygiene, and may feel that nothing they do is good enough for anyone, especially themselves.

Self-dislike is seen in those who don't particularly care too much for themselves. They don't necessarily hate themselves, but they do not find themselves fun to be around, mostly when they are alone. Others may find them enjoyable because of the disguise this person puts on to make others believe they are great, but they do not like to be alone because they don't want to be alone with their unloving thoughts.

Self-complacency is when you don't care enough to think about your personal growth, yourself in any particular way, or if others like or love you. It may sometimes feel like a numbness inside of yourself when you feel like you are going with the flow, but you aren't going along with anything really. You may work a great job, have a family and friends, but no one really gets to know the real you because you don't care enough for them to.

Self-like is when you are dating yourself, and having so much fun doing it! You are getting to know yourself more and more, and making time for self-care. You are learning how to set boundaries, and stick to them even when it seems so hard. You are recognizing what relationships are growing, and which ones are not. You are saying YES more to living your life in a way that feels good to you, and are getting comfortable with saying NO to things you don't want to do or that don't feel good for you.

Self-love is when you are for real in your flow! You love life, you love your life, and you love yourself so gosh darn much! You make decisions that you know are healthy for you and those you love. You make choices that reflect how much you respect and honor the boundaries you have created for your personal growth, mental health, and overall peace. You pour time into your overall health:

mental, emotional, spiritual, and physical. You love yourself enough to know what situations you will not put yourself in, and when it's time to say goodbye to someone or something.

Before you continue reading, I want to remind you that there is no shame or judgment to being on any part of the spectrum that is not self-love. It is important to recognize where you are, so you know where you want to make changes. Self-awareness is one of the greatest ways we can make progress on our healing journey, because we are taking an honest look at who we are, how we show up, and what we want most out of our lives. As long as you are willing to do the work, you will not be stuck in self-loathing, self-dislike, or self-complacency. I personally know many women who have been on various parts of the spectrum, and have still made it to self-love. Heck, I am one of those women! I was in a self-loathing stage that eventually progressed to self-dislike. Yay, for progress! Then I graduated to self-complacency. When I started to take an honest look at my life, invest in the support I needed, and get to know the real me, I began to like myself. It took some time, but soon I was able to love myself. Truly, deeply love myself. That is what my hope is for every single person. Living this life isn't as sweet when we don't love who we are in this life.

I want to invite you to take some time to think about where you are on the spectrum right now. Next, determine where you want to be on the spectrum. Use the real-life stories, inspirational nuggets, and straight talk in this book to help you stock up your Self-Love Toolbox. Think about the purpose of a toolbox. You may have one for your vehicle needs, and maybe one you use for repairs in your home.

When I moved into my first apartment with my young daughter, I ordered this cute purple toolbox from one of the home shopping magazines where you call in your order, and this box included tools with fun purple hand grips on each tool. It had a hammer, screwdriver, wrench, nails, and other basic toolbox items. I remember thinking that by having it I was prepared for any minor home repairs I would need to make. It was only my daughter and me who lived there, so I was responsible for making sure everything was OK. I could not rely on family, friends, or my landlord to come over every time I needed something minor fixed. I had to learn that there would be situations, repairs, and life challenges that I would have to figure out on my own, and there wouldn't be time to be the victim in my own life story. I had to get my toolbox to help me with home repairs. I eventually also figured out that I have a toolbox for life that I need to fill up to prepare for the unexpected, and give me the peace of mind that I have extra help when necessary.

Every part of this book may not be for you; however, there will be pieces that will speak directly to you. When that happens, think of them as additional tools for your Self-Love Toolbox. You get to determine what tools you want that are non-negotiables, what tools are good to have but may not be used often, and what tools people have passed down to you that have helped them and which now can maybe help you. Keep in mind that we cannot fill up our toolbox alone, and please know that it's OK to ask to borrow tools from others as well as ask others to provide some to you that you cannot get on your own. Having a toolbox is important, but not everyone needs the same tools. Are you open to adding a few more items to your Self-Love Toolbox?

Once you are done reading this entire book, I want to encourage you to go back to the Self-Love Spectrum and see if the meter has changed a bit for you and if you have a better understanding of where you are and how to get to where you want to be. Even if you feel you are already at the self-love point, is there a way you can love yourself a little bit more? Don't forget, when we are growing in love with ourselves, it strengthens our relationships with others, gives us more confidence to explore life the way we truly desire, and have more joy and peace within us. Isn't that enough to get that meter moving a bit more to true self-love? Of course it is!

THE R.A.W. SELF-LOVE SPECTRUM

|———————————+———————————+———————————+———————————|

SELF-LOATHING   SELF-DISLIKE   SELF-COMPLACENCY   SELF-LIKE   SELF-LOVE

Where do you feel you are on this Self-Love Spectrum, and why?

_____

_____

_____

_____

_____

_____

_____

_____

_____

_____

_____

_____

_____

_____

CHAPTER ONE

SELF-WORTH

IS THIS REALLY HOW
LIFE IS TURNING OUT?

DEFINITION

Psychologists define self-worth as, "an individual's evaluation of himself or herself as a valuable, capable human being deserving of respect and consideration. Positive feelings of self-worth tend to be associated with a high degree of self-acceptance and self-esteem" (https://dictionary.apa.org/self-worth n.d.).

I would like to add to this definition that self-worth is the way we value ourselves, our health, our lifestyle, the relationships we choose to be a part of, and how we show up for ourselves and others. Ultimately, self-worth comes down to one question: What do you think you are worth?

My client, Shanna, went through the most challenging time of her life, a situation she thought would completely break her. The experience really made her question her worth in so many ways. Here's what she had to say.

I met a guy at work that I really started to like. We started dating and eventually were married. In the beginning everything was wonderful, and we really had fun together. Things were great for a while, and I thought I had found my forever person. I had a daughter at the time I met him who was three years old, so making sure I was with the right guy not just for me but for her was important to me. Her biological father wasn't in her life, so my new husband became more of a father figure to her. After being together for a while, I discovered he was cheating on me. Along with cheating on me, he became mentally and emotionally manipulative. I would confront him about his cheating, and he would turn the blame around on me to take the focus off of what he was doing. If I wore makeup or dressed up, he would tell me I looked like a whore. He would ask me why I'm dressed up to go out, when I needed to be at home. He tried to control most parts of my life.

Everything got worse when I became pregnant with my twins. I was depressed during my pregnancy, and after giving birth to my boys the postpartum depression set in and I felt even worse. I found out that while I was giving birth to my babies that he was with the woman he was cheating on me with. I couldn't believe he did that! While I was at the hospital giving birth to his babies, he was out being with someone else. I felt unworthy, lost, unloved, and really started to believe that I would never be treated the way I wanted to be.

I did stay with him even though he was cheating on me. People would tell me often that I couldn't make it on my own with three kids, and that I needed to stay with him. Guess what? I believed them. He continued to cheat, and I continued to stay stressed, depressed, and exhausted. I felt I wasn't worthy of being loved, and I felt I would never be happy. I finally got the courage to think about leaving, but actually leaving him didn't happen when I thought it would. Once his father passed away, he started drinking alcohol a lot. I remember one day I came home and found him passed out drunk while our children were walking around the house unsupervised. I knew this wasn't a healthy environment for me or my kids, and I also knew I had to figure a way out of this situation.

Once his mom passed, he started drinking even more. Our marriage wasn't a marriage at all. We weren't sleeping in the same bed, we weren't really talking to each other, and we definitely weren't enjoying being around one another. Whenever he did speak to me, his words were mean and meant to make me feel low, which they did. Throughout the relationship I felt so stuck, and I truly believed I couldn't make it on my own with my three children. I believed people when they told me I had to stay with him, because I could not raise my children on my own. I could not believe that this was my life, and I was so emotionally exhausted every single day. I would go to work and cry almost daily. One day, I talked to my female boss about what was going on at home and asked her when I would know that I was for sure done and when it was going to get better for me. And she replied, "When that time comes, you'll have all the signs that it's time to leave." I knew one thing for sure, and that was that my three children loved me and I loved them. I had to leave him before something worse happened.

When I told him I was leaving him, he threatened to kill himself if I did. He was still great at manipulating me, but I was trying to be stronger than his manipulation. My life and my kids' well-being depended on my being strong. Looking back on that time in my life, I did blame him for everything, but I also blamed myself because there were signs all around which I ignored that he was constantly cheating and mistreating me, and I also kept believing what others were telling me that I couldn't make it on my own. And, if I'm being really honest, I wanted to keep my family together and I didn't want my husband to go out and have children with other women if I chose to leave him. Admitting to that doesn't make me feel good, but that was the truth back then.

I prayed to God and asked for a sign that I would be OK if I left him. I received several signs, and this time I was going to pay attention to them. My kids and I moved in with my mom so I could save up some money, so eventually we could make a life without him. During this time, he was begging me to come back and promised me that he would change, but I knew he was a serial cheater and I couldn't allow my daughter to believe this was acceptable behavior for anyone to treat her the way he was treating me.

We were separated for a few years before the divorce was final. By the time the divorce was finalized I felt mad, frustrated, and I blamed him for breaking up our family. I can admit during that time I was a blamer, but I never looked at my actions. I felt lost as a mother, and honestly felt completely lost all over. I could never see myself forgiving him, nor did I feel he deserved my forgiveness. I remember leaving the courthouse, and he apologized to me and told me it was his fault and not mine, but I still felt anger for a long time afterwards. His apology could not repair the years of mistreatment, and I recognized I was also angry at myself for staying so long.

We moved into a two-bedroom apartment with a loft and made our own home. My boys had the loft as their bedroom, my daughter had her own room, and I had mine. It was great having our own place without him, but nothing else was getting better for me during that time. I started having unhealthy habits and would drink more than I should have just to numb myself. I remember being passed out drunk one night, and I woke up to a message for an opportunity to be a part of a company. This was a low point in my life, and I had prayed for a sign about what to do. The message I received to join this company felt like the sign I had prayed for, but did I believe I was worth it?

There are so many parts of Shanna's story that sound like other women's stories I have personally heard. That's the thing, so many of our stories sound the same; however, the ending doesn't have to be. I definitely could relate to parts of her story. When I was in a relationship with someone who was emotionally and mentally abusive, I felt stuck, confused, and embarrassed. My daughter was so young, and I had people (mind you, these were people who knew a good amount of what was going on) tell me to stay with him and work it out. When it became physically abusive, I knew that if I didn't leave, I wouldn't live much longer. Listen, that manipulation is real, and people tend to underestimate it and instead judge the person in the situation without knowing the full story. What part(s) can you relate to?

_____

_____

_____

_____

_____

_____

_____

_____

_____

_____

Now, let's talk about ways to identify how you may view your self-worth.

Statements that a woman may say when she views her self-worth in a negative or un-loving way:

* I am nothing compared to that person.
* Is this really how my life is turning out?
* I think I'm going to be alone forever.
* Nothing good ever happens for me.
* I have to work 24/7 in order to make the money I need, and it's still not enough.
* What's the point of living?
* I suck at being a mom.
* I don't deserve to feel good.
* No matter what I do, it never seems to be enough.
* Maybe I was just born unlucky.

Read those statements and questions above and ask yourself how many of those sound like you. None of them? A few of them? If it's "a few of them" or "literally all of them," then this chapter is definitely for you! Sure, we have all experienced times when we may not have felt good enough for something or someone, or that we did not deserve our deepest desires. The issue comes in when this tends to be your process of thinking on a daily basis, or more times than not. Let's get down to it and talk about what self-worth is really about, how it plays a role in our lives and our relationships, and how we can increase our own self-worth so we can LIKE ourselves so much more than we do right now.

Do you feel that your life and overall health is price-less beyond measure?

Do you believe that your skills and what you bring to the table are valuable and would be an incredible asset to any employer, or for your own business venture?

Do you believe that you are worthy of having healthy, loving, and supportive relationships with friends, family, and your intimate partner(s)?

Or do you feel that you are worth very little—or even that you are worthless?

During one of the times my mom came to visit me in Florida, we were having a conversation about what ways we wanted to work on to love ourselves more, and we dived into the topic of self-worth. My mom told me she didn't feel she struggled with self-worth, and in the same conversation told me how she doesn't take care of her health the way she knows she should. I asked her how is *not* taking care of her health valuing her self-worth. She responded by saying she originally didn't see how not taking care of her health was con-nected to her self-worth, but she can now see how it is.

Let's use another example. Think about when you go into a store, and you see a shirt you think would look flattering on you. You may check the price tag, and there will be different thoughts that may flow through your mind about the price of that top. One of those thoughts may be to ask if that shirt is worth the price on the tag. You may try it on to help you make the decision. You may compare the quality of the fabric to other shirts in the store or stores where you may have seen a similar shirt. You may ask yourself if this is something you can afford to purchase at this time. Out of all of the thoughts you may have, the two that may stand out the most are, "Is this shirt worth buying?" and/or "Do I deserve a shirt like this?" The answer is YES!!! Yes, you do deserve a shirt like that, and any other shirt you want! It's worth buying it if you want it, and it makes you feel empowered, beautiful, sexy, successful, fun, or whatever feeling you have when you look at yourself in the dressing room mirror! You are worth having what you want!

Think about the relationships you are currently in. Your friendships, relationships with family members, relationships with people you may work with or do business with, and intimate relationship(s).

Do you feel respected in those relationships? Do you feel seen and heard in those relationships? Are you in relationships that make you feel liked and loved? Are you honest in those relationships about your needs, boundaries, and desires?

Or do you feel cheated, disrespected, unheard, and unseen in some or all of those relationships? Do you feel you cannot create boundaries in fear that the person or people may reject you? Are you experiencing any form of abuse in any of your relationships, but would you rather stay in that relationship because you feel you are not worth anything better?

I know that someone reading this may feel a little defensive right now. You may be thinking, "Denise, I do have good self-worth! I like myself! I know I am worth a lot!" Ask yourself if that is actually true, and if your behavior backs up your claims of having good or great self-worth.

Maybe you have a habit of allowing people to text, call, or interrupt you constantly, and as a result, you're not able to get what you need done. You may allow other people's needs to take priority over your own. For example: you have a deadline to meet for work or you have a spinning class you signed up for, and you answer a call from your friend who wants to complain about the same issue they have had for months with no changes happening whatsoever. The entire time you want to let them know that you have some work that has to get done, or that you are about to miss a class you were really excited about because it was going to help you de-stress, but instead you continue to listen and put that friend before yourself. Now, don't get me wrong. I am all about helping out others; however, when someone is taking advantage of your time, your kindness, or your energy—it is no longer about helping them and becomes about boundary challenges. These are behaviors that reflect, "I don't believe that my time is worth much, and my needs don't really matter." These behaviors are indicative of low self-worth.

A woman who does not recognize her self-worth will most likely be in victim mode. If you're feeling called out right now, please know that this is not to put you down. Raise your hand if you have at one time been in victim mode. Just so you know, I raised my hand. Victim mode is something that may have been modeled to you as you were growing up. Maybe you saw someone get pity for something they were going through, and you watched how that person got deeper into their own self-pity. You may have witnessed that person receiving attention, because of what they were going through. That may have planted a seed in your head of what you're supposed to do.

Or, maybe you watched someone constantly tell themselves or say out loud how they could not do something. There was no way they could get that promotion at work. They couldn't afford a new car like their neighbors. They would not get asked to the school dance because they weren't as attractive or popular as other students. Maybe someone told you directly that you could not be something because you were not smart enough, and that based on your grades, you would never be anything special in life. Maybe someone told you that the only way to make it in life was to work hard, be the best, and suck up to those above you. Whatever it is, that was then, and this is now. You have the right to change your beliefs, especially if those beliefs are helping you to grow into the person you desire to be. FYI, the person you are desiring to be is already within you. It's just time to let YOU shine through all of the murky stuff. We can do that together.

Let's talk about what happens when you downplay your self-worth. If you do not value yourself, you will allow anyone or anything to come into your life and that includes people, places, and things that do not belong in your life. This may completely resonate with you, or some of you may feel this applies to only a few select areas in your life, and there will be those of you who feel you have grown through this already and you are on the high side of the self-worth meter! Either way, let's take a little road trip into what could happen when we do not recognize our true self-worth.

If you do not feel you are worthy of feeling good daily, having blessings and miracles in your life, having the type of income you desire, being in relationships that are respectful and loving, and living the life that you may dream of, you are wasting this precious gift of your life. Will you allow me to be blunt for a minute please? Yes? Thank you!

If you keep saying you are not worthy of something, you are telling others that you are not worthy, which is exactly how they will treat you, and that will play into your belief that you are indeed not worthy. You don't get to be mad at others for treating you the same way you treat yourself. If you want people to treat you like someone who knows their self-worth, you must first start acting like a person who knows their self-worth.

First let me say, you are not alone if this is a challenging area in your life. Many women struggle with their self-worth. The messages you received that made you believe you are not worthy could have come from family members, teachers, society, books, TV shows, or maybe from places that you didn't recognize. It most definitely can be challenging recognizing your self-worth when society puts it smack dead in your face what you "should" do or be in order to feel worthy of anything you want in your life. And lo and behold, those who choose to do anything different may be made fun of by a friend or two, bullied on social media, talked about at family holiday dinners, or frowned upon by their higher-ups at work. You get to do what you want to do that feels good to you! Is it too soon to remind you again that this is your one known life on this earth, so why the heck wouldn't you live it the way you want to? It's not too late, so don't beat yourself up that you could have started this new self-worth journey earlier. You're doing it now, and that's part of what matters. What really matters is that you truly start to make yourself a priority without feeling guilty about it. You matter! I'm telling you that you do, and I will gladly tell you as many times as you need to hear it!

The cost of ignoring this issue is bigger than you may recognize. This will cost you seeing your life in a way that brings you peace and harmony. This will cost you relationships that will be loving, understanding, and enjoyable on both sides. This will cost you fulfilling all of your dreams. The ultimate price is having to replay all of your regrets at the end of your life. Is that how you treat a special gift that is only meant for you? This gift of life that you are choosing to make less than because you are holding on to false beliefs that you are not worthy to have a better life, better circumstances, better career, better relationships, better outlook on life. When will you stop being in victim mode and come out as the brave person who is ready to live life on purpose? What if you start right now?

I asked Shanna what her challenge of having low self-worth cost her, and this is what she had to say.

Having low self-worth cost me years of unnecessary mental and emotional pain, and too many times feeling like I was a bad mom. I lost out on having healthy relationships with friends and family, because I felt I wasn't worthy of them. I felt my self-worth was dependent on being validated by others liking and accepting me. Comparing myself to others as a friend, a wife, and a mom was the norm for me, and doubting myself was a regular occurrence. My confidence seemed to be tied into what others thought about my appearance, so that sometimes made me feel self-conscious about how I looked. Worst of all, I felt I wasn't worthy of loving myself.

Let's take a few deep breaths right here. Breathe in and breathe out. Repeat two more times please. Do you know how many women would feel judged if they were in Shanna's shoes? Feeling like you cannot leave a bad situation, and then when you do you still feel lost and unhappy? You may be afraid to tell people what's really going on in your life, to admit that you truly don't know what to do, and you feel that you're supposed to know. Here is just a little dose of loving reality: we are not meant to do it all, know it all, or be all. It is OK to feel lost, because there are ways to be found. It is OK to feel stuck, because there are ways to get unstuck. It is OK to feel unsure about your next step, because there are ways to get support to help you figure it out.

What if I told you that you could change your beliefs around what self-worth means to you, and increase your self-worth meter so you can view yourself in a new and loving way? How different would your life be if you started to value yourself so much that de-valuing yourself was a complete non-negotiable? Would your relationships change? Would the way you show up for your family and friends change? Would the words, thoughts, and actions you have for yourself change? Let me help you with this answer—

YES!!!!! All that and then some will change for you! Keep reading to see what happened with Shanna when she started changing how she viewed her self-worth.

Remember that message I received to join that company? Well, I did, and it helped me in so many ways. I started helping other women feel empowered and that actually helped to empower me. When I made changes for myself, my daughter started to notice my growth and could see how I was thriving in areas I once felt I was shriveling up in. My **three** children have watched me work hard to create a better life for them, sometimes with **two** jobs, and even through the extremely hard times when I felt I wasn't worthy of a better life. That belief had to change, and I had to find support to help me. I wanted to remind my children they are worthy and loved, so I had to remind myself of the same thing. I felt I couldn't be loved because I was divorced, a single mom, and only experienced relationships that weren't loving. I had to find my self-worth and find healthy ways to feel better about myself. I knew I needed to heal, and I wasn't 100 percent sure how. I would listen to motivational speakers and Audibles, and attend inspiring conferences, but I needed more. I knew I had to forgive my ex, but I didn't know I also needed to forgive myself first.

I hired Denise as my mindset coach, and I started to apply the tools she gave me to learn how to love myself in ways I didn't know. I learned how to not bring my past into my present, and instead to learn from my past to not repeat past feelings, thoughts, and behaviors that were not loving. For me to receive the love I prayed for, I first had to learn how to love myself in all ways and on all levels. Hiring Denise has been the best investment I have made that was just for me, and just the idea of having a coach was proof that I believed I truly was worthy of more. More love, support, desires fulfilled, peace, and joy. Because I made these changes for myself, my daughter knows how to treat herself, and how to be treated by others. My boys know how to treat themselves and how to treat others. I want my children to know love, receive love, and give love. I thank God every day I am not where I used to be.

Shanna, I love you and you are 10000000 percent worthy of everything you want! We are all worthy of everything we want! We just have to believe it, because no one can believe it for us. That's an inside job. You can get support from a therapist, a coach, a mentor, a shaman, a non-judgmental buddy, but none of it matters if you are not willing to make the changes to believe you are worthy of love, peace, joy, success, or whatever it is you want most!

When a woman has strong self-worth, everyone knows it, and most importantly she knows it. That woman will have the strength and courage to step away from relationships that are not loving and kind, because she knows she is worth being in relationships with people who value her and see her for the incredible being that she is. This woman goes after her dreams, and does not stay in a job that does not bring her joy. A good or great paycheck/salary is one thing, but feeling fulfilled and pure joy with what you do to earn your income is on a different level. Guess what? You deserve that.

Now, if you're reading this and thinking, "Denise, I am not that smart. I don't have degrees coming out of a fancy briefcase. Who is going to support this wild idea I have? I don't know enough people to help me get started, it's too risky trying something without a guarantee, and I don't even know if my dream job is something I can actually do because of x, y, and z." PLEASE, stop that noise right now! Let me get cheesy for a minute. If you can dream it, you can become it! Seriously, nothing is guaranteed anyway, so why not just go for what you want? I'm actually chuckling to myself as I was typing that last question, because that is so much easier said than done.

Here's the deal, when we value our self-worth, we know we are worth any risk, dream, idea, and lifestyle. Let me remind you (and heads up I may or may not say this a few more times throughout this book): you have one known life on this earth that you are currently living, and you get to choose how you live it. Your self-worth plays a big part in how you view your life and what you believe you deserve in this lifetime.

What goes hand in hand with self-worth is creating boundaries. When you know what you will and will not accept into your life you create boundaries to solidify that. Creating boundaries is not always easy, and if it was, more people would be doing it. I know you've been waiting for a secret sauce to increase your self-worth. Well, one of the main ingredients to that secret sauce—which, by the way, isn't a secret—is setting boundaries and sticking to them.

Here's how to start setting boundaries:

Step 1: What do you want in every area of your life?

Your Overall Health:

_____

_____

_____

_____

Relationships with Others:

_____

_____

_____

_____

Work:

_____

_____

_____

_____

Other Area(s):

_____

_____

_____

Step 2: What are you willing (and not willing) to do to have that in your life?

_____

_____

_____

_____

_____

_____

_____

_____

_____

_____

_____

_____

_____

_____

_____

_____

_____

_____

Step 3: Dig deep into your soul and ask yourself, who do you want in your life, and who is draining you like a thirsty vampire?

_____

_____

_____

_____

_____

_____

_____

_____

_____

_____

_____

_____

_____

_____

_____

_____

_____

_____

_____

Step 4: What will happen if you don't take the first step and actually apply it to your life? What will happen if you do take the first step and apply it to your life? My loving reminder to you—please be honest and take responsibility for this part.

_____

_____

_____

_____

_____

_____

_____

_____

_____

_____

_____

_____

_____

_____

_____

_____

_____

_____

_____

_____

Let's use an example from Shanna's story.

Shanna knew she had to get out of her marriage, because it was draining her to the point where she felt she was losing herself. She knew the consequences of what could happen if she stayed with her husband, and she knew what could happen if she left her husband. She knew both situations would be challenging, but she also knew that the challenging solution of leaving him would eventually lead to a life out of depression and darkness. She had to forget what people were telling her—that she wouldn't make it on her own as a single mother—and she had to take charge anyway. This was one of the times Shanna had to set some clear boundaries for herself, her family, and others who wanted to give her direction. She had allowed some of her family members and other people outside of her family to influence the decisions she needed to make for her and her children. Shanna decided the boundaries she needed to set first were clarifying what she would and would no longer accept from her husband, and what information she would and would not share or take from her family and other concerned people.

When I asked Shanna what major changes she discovered internally and externally while going through her transformational journey, increasing her self-worth and self-love, and being a boundary setting queen, this is what she said:

* I've gotten stronger with finding love within myself.
* I have tools to help me release a lot more pain instead of holding onto it.
* I have learned to love and be kinder to others.

* I am no longer holding onto anger and resentment, and now I'm happier. That feels good to say!
* I have more joy within me.
* Overall, I have more confidence!
* I empower my children and my clients, because I feel more empowered.
* My business is thriving and I'm earning more money, because I'm more confident in what I do.
* My team has noticed the changes within me, and comment on them quite often. This has also encouraged them to want to seek support to help them on their self-love journey.
* I feel more connected with my children, and our communication with each other is better.
* My daughter and I have date nights, which has helped us become closer as she's getting older.
* People tell my children they are blessed to have me as a mom, because others now see me as a strong, loving, and compassionate person.

THIS IS BEAUTIFUUUUUUUULLLLLLLL!!!!! When we work on ourselves it absolutely, positively helps those around us! Just like when we are a whole hot mess, it absolutely negatively affects those around us. Soooo, which way are you choosing?

Some statements a woman who knows her worth may say:

* I know I deserve better than this, so I am going to do what I need to do in order to have better.
* This relationship is not something I can be a part of any longer, because it feels more hurtful than loving, and I deserve to feel loved in my relationships.

* I may not know what this next business move will bring me, but I do know that what I am doing right now is no longer working for me.
* I know I deserve good things to happen, and I also have the control to make good things happen for me.
* I may be a mom, a life partner, a daughter, and a slew of other titles, but most importantly I am a person who deserves to be happy.
* Because I respect myself, I am not going to allow you to talk to me or treat me in a disrespectful way.

A woman who knows her self-worth will surround herself with people who also know their self-worth. She will do loving things for herself that benefit her overall health: emotional health, mental health, spiritual health, and physical health. She will not blame the past for her present way of life. She will take charge to learn from her past and use it as a stepping stone to help her grow in her present life. She will get support, she will spend time alone getting to know herself, and she will talk to herself like she is the most special person she knows.

She will take action in her life, and not play the victim role. Making yourself the victim sends the message that everyone and everything else has control over your life, and you are just sitting waiting for the next shoe to drop. You are not the victim. You are the powerful, loving, and creative being you were born to be!

A LOVING R.A.W. MESSAGE FROM SHANNA TO YOU:

You are worthy and deserving of being loved and treated with respect. If you're feeling lost or stuck, find someone to really open up to. What helped me find my way was not through a therapist, but a mindset coach who helped me find ME again. Having my mindset coach taught me ways to feel loved, validated, and worthy with transformative exercises and tools. There are many avenues of support out there, and you just have to find the one that works best for you. It may not seem like you'll ever get out of what you're going through right now, but trust me, there will be a time such as this that hopefully my story will help YOU know there is always a new beginning—a fresh new start!

SELFIE TIME!

Here are some fun steps that can be helpful on your self-worth journey!

1. Stop what you're doing and take a quick selfie with your phone. Please do not change your hair or clothes, and do not give in to the need to put on makeup. Also, please don't get distracted with texts or social media notifications that may have popped up on your phone while you were reading this chapter. You can check those later. This time is for you right now.

2. Make that selfie your screensaver and keep it as your screensaver for at least the next ten days. You know that I have special powers, and I know that you may have just had a thought

that you were not going to do that. Let me ask you this. What is your screensaver now? Is it a picture of you with someone else, a quote that you love, or maybe something completely different? Either way that screen saver (if you have one) means something to you. This book is all about YOU, and loving your SELFIE. Aren't you just as important (really more so, but let's move on) as whatever or whoever else is on your screen saver? Also, just in case you forgot, you can always change the screen-saver back.

3. Give yourself grace. Every time you pick up your phone and you see that beautiful face of yours, remind yourself that with each passing day you are learning how to add value to yourself and to your life. This is not an overnight process. This will take time, and you are worth that time, so give yourself grace during this time.

You showed yourself some love already just by reading this chapter. Whether you feel that increasing your self-worth is a big ole' challenge for you, or you feel that this is only a challenge for you in some areas, or maybe you feel this is not a challenge for you at all— take whatever nuggets you can from this chapter and help yourself or help someone else.

NINA HONIGMAN'S SELF-WORTH STORY

WHEN WE KNOW WE DESERVE BETTER... AND WE GO FOR IT! HERE IS THE JOURNEY OF A WOMAN WHO WENT FROM JUSTIFYING THE LIFE SHE WAS LIVING TO TAKING RESPONSIBILITY FOR HAVING THE LIFE SHE WANTED TO LIVE.

The period in my life when I struggled the most with my self-worth was during my relationship with my boyfriend at that time, who was an alcoholic. He never wanted to make decisions, so I had to make all of the decisions for us. That had me feeling as though I was in a relationship alone. The more time that passed in our relationship the more we seemed to argue, and I felt like I was turning into a controlling person. That was not the way I was before, and I didn't want to be that way then. I wanted a partner who was just as involved as I was, but since he was an alcoholic that wasn't what he could give me. I understood he had a disease, but I also knew I didn't deserve to be in a relationship where I wasn't being fulfilled.

Towards the end of my relationship with my him, I felt I changed into a person I didn't recognize. That was not OK, but I wasn't sure exactly what I needed to do. There was a day we were attending a wedding, and were going to carpool with some of my friends and their spouses. When I got home the day we were leaving for the wedding after being out for a bit, my boyfriend was passed out drunk, but he was "functional." He got in the car for a ride that was several hours long. I was so angry at him, and also embarrassed and frustrated. In my head I knew this couldn't be my life, but I also tried to justify his behaviors and thought maybe things would get better. I loved him so much, so the excuses became something I just had to hold on to, and honestly something I became too familiar with. I also found myself going into hustle mode with work, because I was trying to find validation and love in other ways that I wasn't getting from him.

I decided it was time for me to start working on myself to become better than what I was feeling, and once the inner work began, I started recognizing what the relationships I was in meant in my life and who I was in those relationships. I knew I deserved more in my relationship with whoever I chose to have as a life partner, and in my friendships. I couldn't keep trying to fix people, and I was done asking myself why I was the only one trying to make these relationships work. I was leaning more into self-development and he wasn't. This new outlook on my life flowed into my business. When I realized I was worth having more I started trying more in my business.

I literally had an AHA moment! One day while driving I witnessed a horrible car accident and realized right then and there that I truly deserved more in my life, and I was done making excuses about why things were the way they were. I went home that day and broke up with him. This was two weeks after the wedding fiasco. I wasn't an angry person, so to constantly be angry at him was exhausting and I didn't want to be that way. That helped me make the decision to make the change and eventually leave him. You hear people say life is so short, and when I physically saw it in front of my eyes, I had a WTF moment. I knew I deserved more and I was determined to have it! I always had a boyfriend, so after the breakup I took two years off of dating. This was the perfect time for me to truly and deeply work on me. I wanted to get to know myself more, so I dived into many new ways to discover how to do just that. I started working with a mindset coach (Denise), attended a retreat, started listening to podcasts that benefited my self-love journey, and spent time with people who made me feel good. I can proudly say that I have come a long way, and I am committed to making decisions that benefit my increasing self-worth and the new-found love I have for myself.

Having the challenges of low self-worth cost me:

* Wasted time and energy on people and situations that didn't bring me joy. Also, giving more of myself to people who weren't reciprocating.

Changes that have happened to me and for me since increasing my self-worth:

* It's easier for me to make decisions, because I feel more confident in knowing what I am deserving of, so I go after what I want more. For example, I choose friends that I have similar

values with and friendships that are not just about fun.

* When it comes to work, it has had its challenges with moving to another state; however, because I have a new mindset about what I deserve I know I can have more in my business.

* After taking a two-year break from having a serious relationship I got to a point of knowing what I wanted in a partner after knowing what I wanted for myself.

* I identify what my personal values are in friendships, and when meeting new people, I try to identify those values in other people. I have really leaned into having real conversations and not superficial ones, so I know if I want to continue spending time with those people.

* I am now with a partner who matches my values. We make decisions together, and we plan life together. He has my back and I have his.

* I feel confident in my abilities to do my job really well, and in making decisions for my business.

* I don't have it all figured out, and I even feel confident saying that. I know I will figure out what I want and need as I continue living in the way that feels good to me.

* I started thinking about my legacy, so thinking beyond my relationships, working, paying bills, and day to day routines. This is a huge mental shift for me!

A LOVING R.A.W. MESSAGE FROM NINA TO YOU:

Have more loving self-talk. Say your goals out loud. Listen to podcasts that tell you how worthy you are, and keep listening until you believe it. Stop saying ONE DAY and start doing the work. This is not an overnight process, so find ways that will help you grow. For me that was putting in work with a coach, and listening to positive influences through podcasts and reading books to help me improve myself in various areas.

Whether you're stuck in a relationship or a job that is no longer serving you, don't wait to get out. I wish someone would have asked me during my darkest times, "What are you waiting for, Nina?" That's what the car crash that I witnessed did for me. It shook me, and made me think about how life is not guaranteed, so why not start today and make the changes. It's OK if you don't know the next step right away. Lean into what feels good, and make a list of things you never did but you thought would be cool to do alone. You will naturally meet people along the way who will want to do the things you want to do. Explore different styles of self-development to see what works best for you.

Take breaks to celebrate your progress, no matter how small you think it is. A step forward is a step forward. It's also OK if you fail. It's a part of the process of growing. It's OK to be uncomfortable.

CHAPTER TWO

SELF-VALIDATION

IS THIS GOOD ENOUGH?

DEFINITION

According to *Psychology Today,* self-validation is, "The act of accepting our own internal experience, including our thoughts and feelings."

Personally, I also believe that self-validation is being confident enough to acknowledge, appreciate, and celebrate what we want, desire, and accomplish without outside confirmation.

ere is a real-life example of what seeking outside validation is from one of my clients, Ashley Mclauren Walker.

I remember working my business within a company for several years, and thinking, "I know what I want and I know how to do it." I knew I could do more in my business to make it better than it was, but the way I knew how to do it was to hustle, hustle, hustle. I compared myself to others in the company and knew I could do better than what I currently was doing. I remember during the time my family and I were moving into a new house I had also broken my foot. You would think having a broken foot and a big move would slow me down a bit, but I was still in hustle mode trying to make my business better than before, and in all honesty wanting my business to be better than anyone else's in the company.

I wanted to prove that where I came from wasn't my story. I had two loving parents, but I didn't always feel supported growing up. So, I felt the need to prove I could do anything without outside support. Even though I was seeking outside validation, I didn't want outside support. I had this mentality that not only could I do whatever I wanted, but I could do it better than anyone else. I remember being in Zumba, and learning the routine so well that I did it better than the instructor. That played over into other areas in my life, including the company I was a part of for years. I had to prove I could be the best and be at the top, where the majority of the people were not. During that time of my life, I was so deep in my s%&t that I didn't understand this need that I had to prove I could do things, that it actually took away so much.

The people I loved were a priority, but my business was my real priority. I justified the sacrifices my family had to make in order for me to build my business. The sacrifices my husband and children had to make were justified in my mind by me building a hefty bank account. I justified myself being away working most nights by giving my time away from home a fun name for my husband and sons— father-and-son date nights. Looking back, there wasn't a joint effort. I was out working on my business, and not home working on my family. It was never my intention to be one of the best in the company, it was my intention to be THE best in the company. I didn't want to be in the top 5 percent, I wanted to be the top ONE, and I would justify anything to get there. Then one day I decided I didn't want to build someone else's dream, I wanted to build my own. That's when I realized this was going to take some work, and I could no longer live by the belief that I didn't want outside support. It was time to make some changes, because my family and I had sacrificed enough.

Am I the only one who can relate to Ashley's story? I doubt it! I remember working for a particular company while working one to two other jobs, and being in straight hustle mode 24/7. I hardly ever saw my friends, attended family events, or just had fun outside of my work environment. The time I missed out on in my daughter's younger years was justified because I was making a living for us, or that's what I was telling myself because that is seriously what I believed to be true. I was so fearful of being labeled a statistic—black single mom, living paycheck to paycheck, government health insurance, no savings account, not with my daughter's father, etc., etc.—that I worked around the clock to prove to others that I wasn't just those labels of people who couldn't hack it. I was so dang worried about how others saw me, that I was stressed the heck out every single day. That was no way to live, and what kind of example was I showing my daughter? Not a great one during that time. Ashley's story and my story are not very different from many women we know. This book is never to bash on men, because I do believe we are all equal humans; however, I do want to point out that the guilt of working seems to be something women internalize more so than men. I am ONLY basing this on the people I know, studies I have read, and research I have dived into. Of course, there are always different ideas, beliefs, and truths around this topic; however, sticking to this idea that women do internalize feeling guilt over working, is that something you do? And if so, are you doing it for your own self-validating reasons, "I work hard so I can afford to take family vacations twice a year and solo trips every year for my birthday," or for outside validation?

When a woman tends to seek outside validation over self-validation, these are some statements she may think or say:

* If I work harder, then maybe they will notice me.
* I am not qualified to go after that opportunity.

* Let me ask (insert a person other than yourself here) if I am good enough to go for it (whatever that "IT" is that could be fun, life changing or just something you really want to do for your own reasons).
* I really want to wear my new yellow top to that event, but maybe if I dress more conservative people will take me seriously. I'll just wear my navy-blue dress instead.
* If I earn that award, then I'll know that I'm successful.
* If I do it my way, she/he/they may be upset with me for not doing it their way.
* I usually ask multiple people for advice and feedback before I make a decision.
* Nobody "liked" or commented on my latest Instagram and/or Facebook post, and honestly, it really bummed me out and I started to doubt myself.
* I'm successful, but I'll never be as successful as _____ .
* I didn't get the shout out I was expecting. Maybe I didn't do as good of a job as I thought.

Which of the above statements sound familiar to you? Which ones have been on replay in your mind recently? Which one caused an emotional trigger?

Question time: why do you ignore your trusted and loving inner companion, a.k.a your own personal intuition?

Let's take a moment to reflect on our pasts. I like to say that we can visit our past to get answers to our questions; however, living in our past is where we get into trouble. So, with that being said, if you take a few quiet moments to think back to when you stopped trusting your intuition, you may feel more confident creating the belief that you can start trusting your intuition. We are all born with instincts about how to protect ourselves, and through our upbringings, things we are taught from others through society, family, friends, school, etc., we start to bring in everyone else's beliefs, and somewhere along the way we forget that we have an inner guide that knows us best.

Let's take a few minutes together and think back to a time you can remember when you questioned something you wanted to do. Maybe it was wanting to wear a particular outfit you thought would look amazing on you, but someone in your family or one of your friends told you that it didn't look good with your figure. Now, the belief you had about this fun outfit you were excited to wear has now shifted to a belief that you can never wear an outfit like that, because others said it didn't look good on you.

Let's go a different route, and think back to a time when you may have told someone about an incredible idea you had for what you want to do to earn money—starting a business that can make a difference in your world and others, joining a circus as the person who swings from those high beams and catches another human, or something else, and you were so pumped about this idea you could see it clear as day. Every time you thought about this idea you would smile so big, and your heart would even beat a little faster from the excitement! After sharing this idea with this trusted person, they burst your bubble in what they felt was a loving way by sprinkling doubt and insecurity glitter all over your dreams, and suddenly your high energy beliefs around this idea had shifted into believing this dream may not be as good as you originally thought. My goodness!! Why do we do this????

Sure, you may have had people in your life who also wanted to protect you, and most times they did so in the way they believed was best. Was it always right? Sometimes. As a baby we definitely are at the grace and mercy of others, and as we get older, we may sometimes feel we are still at the grace and mercy of others. This is where the blurred lines come in, when we start to trust everyone else over ourselves. This is also where a trip down Self-Awareness Avenue is crucial to discovering what it is you want and need out of your own life, without others telling you what you want and need. As a functioning adult, you have the power to do so. Do you believe that to be true?

At one of the R.A.W. retreats that I hosted I asked the women if they trusted their intuition, and every single one of them said YES! I then asked them if they always follow through on what their intuition tells them or shows them, and they all said NO! One of the women there said that she sometimes will start to follow through, but then gets scared of what will actually happen so she doesn't go all the way through. In the story Ashley shared with us, she did get to a point where she wanted to start a new business venture, but she was also unsure at first about how to do it or if it could be as successful as what she had built already with her current business. Her intuition told her she would have to get outside support to get the ball rolling, but remember, that was not something Ashley was used to asking for. Her intuition was guiding her, but it took a minute for her to trust in it. Are you like Ashley and the women from that particular retreat? Do you say you trust your intuition to help you make the right decisions, but you feel you are not confident enough to follow through? Is that why you ask everyone for their opinion, suggestion, advice, and belief about what you are meant to do? Why would your parent(s), partner, neighbor, best friend, or the person you just met at the grocery store be able to tell you what is best for you?

Now, don't get me wrong, there are situations where bouncing ideas, asking for advice and suggestions, or getting outside help and support is absolutely necessary. What I'm talking about is when there is something you feel deep in your soul you want to do, want to change, or want to seek more clarity on and you're asking others what to do. You may disagree with me on this, buuuuuuttttttt here it is. No one, and I mean NO ONE, knows you better than you know yourself. You may have people in your life who know you pretty darn well, but do they know ALL of you? Your deep and dark thoughts, secrets, truest wants, desires, and pains (mental, physical, emotional, spiritual); every single feeling you experience, every traumatic and life-altering experience; the thoughts that keep you up at night; the fears and doubts that can sometimes suffocate you; the true depths of the fear you have of not being good enough or not being loved enough; what makes you feel attractive, loved, accepted, and understood? Do they know about that one time you felt so low that you wondered what would happen if you no longer existed, and every single thought, feeling, and experience that led up to that moment? Do they know why that dream of yours that you want to bring into reality is truly so important to you, how your entire life could change for the better, and how it has nothing to do with the reason you're telling people?

Yes, there are people in our lives who know a whole bunch of stuff about us, but there is no way possible that any one person can know every single thing about you. So, with that being said, why would you trust their advice, thoughts, and beliefs over your own inner support guide? It is also important to note here that others' beliefs are shaped by many factors that have nothing to do with how your beliefs were shaped, and how your beliefs may continue to change shape.

The thoughts behind why we feel we need outside validation can come from good and not-so good experiences, which usually stem from our childhood. You may have been a straight-A, Honor Roll student, and were praised for it. Now, you may believe that receiving praise is the same as love, acceptance, and being truly seen and heard. With that same belief in mind, if you do not receive praise for something it can lead to feelings of doubt, insecurities, despair, unworthiness, and disappointment. For some people it can push them into hyperdrive, and now they are doing more than they truly want to just to get recognized for their hard work. Do you find yourself saying things such as, "I love my job/career so much that I don't mind spending every single day working on it, even if I don't have much of a personal/social life. At least I know I'm doing something with meaning. I'll rest when I retire." Listen, I also love what I do for a living, but I love my free time more. You may truly love what you do and feel like it feeds your soul. CONGRATULATIONS!!! Now, ask yourself if you are truly doing what you're doing as hard as you are doing it for your own personal validation, or for the validation, recognition, and acceptance from others. Be honest with yourself, and understand you are not being judged for your honesty.

Here is another example of how a series of childhood experiences may have shaped why you seek outside validation. Were you punished often for your behavior, whether it was because you were told you talked too much, you didn't receive good grades in school, or because you may have been expressive with your actions and been in fights with your siblings or the kids in the neighborhood, or did not always do as you were told by your authority figures? This could have played a role in why you feel you have to be "perfect" in order for others to take you seriously, or be more submissive in order to feel loved, or even feel as though no matter what you do people will only see the not-so great part of you and not the parts of you that you want to shine through.

Here is a spoonful of R.A.W. love—you are capable of trusting yourself to make the right decisions for your life. Your worth is not determined by someone else's praise. Your feelings do not have to make sense to others, as long as they make sense to you. Your dreams and desires are not too big; they may just be too big for others to visualize and that is OK, because they are your dreams and desires—not theirs.

You may be asking yourself if it is common to want validation from others, and the answer is YES! You may want validation from your family, spouse/partner, friends, or boss; however, some people seek outside validation to an unhealthy level. This means some people may rely on others to make them feel good. Some may doubt their skills or abilities if they are not directly told they are doing well. This may also look like obsessively checking your social media posts looking for approval. And it is not uncommon to question your worth if others don't value you the way you want to be valued. I get it! I used to be that way in relationships. I saw this a lot when I was dating and seeking validation that the relationship was going well based on how they felt about it. After going to therapy, I was able to figure out that this stemmed from feeling like I could never please my mother. I compared the way my maternal grandmother showed me love with the way my mother showed me love, and it seemed very different. So, I felt I had to do more and be more to gain my mother's approval. This flowed over into my relationships when I started dating. Thank goodness this was resolved before I got married. UGGGGHHHHH! That would have been a disaster. I am also happy to note that through therapy, growing pains and gains, kumbayas, lots of prayer, hot tea, and patience, my mother and I have a much healthier relationship now.

See, we all have areas of growing, learning, changing, and shedding.

This is the time to be honest with yourself and take ownership of the thoughts you allow in your mind, and to figure out where they came from and what you want to do with them. Remember, you are reading this chapter for a reason. Maybe you are currently feeling challenged in this validation arena, or maybe you have already taken steps to lean more into self-validation and not seeking outside validation. Either way, how would you like to grow in this area?

For those who are seeking outside validation, that need didn't just come out of thin air. It may have come from wanting to please those who raised you, or wanting to stand out in school or sports. That initial praise we received from using the potty for the first time, taking our first step, coloring our first picture that was outside of the lines but still something to cheer about, bringing home a great report card, or learning a new song on our instrument has stuck with us. That praise and recognition did something to us that ignited a fire inside of our spirit that said, "Praise is good, let's get more of it." So, then we go on a quest throughout our lives trying to get more praise, recognition, kudos, likes and hearts on social media, and awards to make us believe we are worthy of praise and our hard work has made us special in the eyes of whoever is giving us the praise. I need to take a quick walk after that AHA moment, because there is so much truth in it.

Listen, I think we all need a moment of silence to think about the little child we once were who just wanted to make EVERYONE else happy, and along the way forgot what made her/him/them happy. Are you the adult version of that child who is still trying to make everyone else happy? Are you still trying to prove yourself, and waiting for others to confirm your greatness? It's OK if the answer is YES, because that doesn't have to stay your answer. Remember, we have access to the power, support, tools (if you actually use them) and love for ourselves to make the changes necessary for our growth and our overall health. The question is WILL you use what is available to you to make the changes?

Excuse me for sounding repetitive because I may say this (or not) a few times throughout this book, but you made the choice to dive into this book for a reason. I would like to go a bit deeper and say that something bigger than you guided you to this book. There is always something or someone working in our favor, and it doesn't matter what you believe in, whether it's God, the universe, nature, your higher self, fish sticks, your imaginary friend Mary, or something else. There is something and/or someone bigger than us, and that entity loves to support us by sending us clear-as-day messages that some of us like to ignore. No judgment, but ummmm, is that you ignoring the messages from your bigger-than-life bestie? If so, stop it!!! You reading this book could be one of those messages, and not skipping over this chapter may for real be a message.

Take a few moments and think about what areas in your life you are seeking outside validation in. Don't rush through this and write down the first thing that sounds good. Be honest here and really think about it, but please don't skip this part. Then write down what it has cost you already by relying on outside validation to make you feel successful, appreciated, or seen.

What has it cost your peace of mind, happiness, and quality of life by feeling as though you need the approval from others in order to take action or feel important?

_____

_____

_____

_____

_____

What will it cost you and those you love if you are not willing to get to the root cause of what has made it difficult for you to experience validation from within?

_____

_____

_____

_____

_____

How has this challenge cost you life changing opportunities, income, healthy relationships, or any part of the quality of your life?

_____

_____

_____

_____

_____

When I asked Ashley what having the challenge of seeking outside validation had cost her, this was her response:

* Relationships that are important to me.
* Things that are more valuable than money.
* There are people I could've had more special times with, but I was more concerned with making something big of myself.
* My mental health is a big one, because for a while I struggled with anxiety.
* I was hard to live with while I was with my former company, which I found out later from my husband. It was really taxing on him, and I believe it had an impact on our relationship that I didn't recognize at the time.
* My grandmother told me I didn't hear anyone. She would tell me I worked too much, but I didn't hear her. I justified my actions.
* The Kool-Aid I was drinking had so much sugar in it, that I couldn't see.
* Making real connections with others.
* Trying to fit in a mold that didn't even really exist.

I bet some of you right now are wishing you had Ashley's phone number to call and ask her how she got out of that mindset, because you are where she was! There is no one-size-fits-all solution; however, it does take changing up how you see yourself and what you believe to be true about yourself.

If you keep reading, Ashley shares what changed for her.

The way I was living wasn't sustainable for me, and what I really mean is the way I was thinking was no longer working for me. Actually, it never was, but that's what I believed for so long. I knew I needed help in changing my ways, and I knew that meant I first had to change within myself. At the time I didn't know about getting a coach, but when I found out that there was a way I could get support to help me with my mindset I was all for it. Through working with my coach, Denise, I started finding new ways to appreciate my life, and feel grateful for what I already had. I started doing different types of work that my coach recommended for my healing, such as journaling, which initially I didn't like. After some time, I understood the purpose of the exercises she gave me, and how it was helping me transform the way I saw myself in my life. One of the journaling exercises she gave me when we first started working together was beginning the day with three things I was thankful for. Instead of focusing on outward people, it made me think inward. Mom guilt was a big thing for me, and I wanted to do everything perfectly with both of my boys and I started to notice that perfectionism was not realistic. My ideas around being the perfect mom were one of the greatest changes I made, but it started with first changing my ideas around perfectionism.

Another breakthrough I had was with my grandmother, who is my biggest supporter in life. Even with her being who she is in my life, we had to get to a level in our relationship of recognizing that the expectations we put on each other were not healthy or helping. For years I felt I was a rebel by doing what I wanted to do, but I also learned guilt words from my upbringing. I was able to let my grandmother know what I needed from her, and let me tell you, I was nervous as nervous could be when I thought about having that conversation with her. You see, I never wanted to disappoint my grandmother, but I got to a point where it wasn't about disappointing her, it was about no longer disappointing myself. I used to think I needed to be a certain way for my grandmother, but once I took those expectations away, we were able to come to an understanding of what we needed from each other.

The universe has a way of creating a beautiful story if we allow it. The whole time I was creating something I thought I wanted, I was actually creating something that I didn't know I wanted. I recognized I didn't really want to want recognition, but it was something I thought I needed. I finally threw away all of my trophies and certificates from past accomplishments. I realized I had twenty-two trophies, which goes to show a few things. Yes, I loved to overachieve, and do the best at everything, but also the fact that I'm telling you I threw those all away shows you that holding onto them was attached to my old ways of thinking that I needed those to prove my worth. My worth has always been based on what someone else thought, or what they gave me to show that worth. Trophies, report cards, paychecks, the amount of money in my bank accounts. My worth was never just about me, it was about what I could do. So, while in the process of doing the work of figuring out who I am, the work was finding the value in what I want.

Now, I do things that are fun. Yes, FUN! It became fun to trust the universe. A big thing that changed was my spirituality, which was another shaky ground for me at a point in time, and one that I battled with because of how I thought others may judge me based on what I was choosing to believe. I'm learning to learn things from myself, and what my relationship with God is like for me. Being a preacher's daughter felt like a tough place to be. But when I go deeper within knowing myself, I realized I get to determine my relationship with spirituality and God. I'm learning to trust if I show up, the money will come. I'm learning to honor my body, whereas in the past, outside opinions would've determined my actions. When you take validation, expectations, opinions out of the question—things have a way of aligning in ways that may surprise you. Sometimes when we are in the mess, we get conflicted about what's right. So, now I am to the point of just doing what feels right. I now know that I had to re-learn how to validate myself and not seek outside validation, and when I think about how far I've come in my growth I can only smile and feel grateful!

Can we take a moment to applaud Ashley please?! I know I am cheering for her, and I always will. I will cheer for any person who takes those unknowing steps to wanting to find the parts of themselves that have been hiding away. Ashley, thank you for trusting in the process, and for trusting me to be a part of it.

I want to share some of my personal favorite parts of Ashley's new-found love and appreciation for her life:

* She spends time baking bread with her boys.
* She takes week-long breaks or longer from social media.
* She quit the job that she put so much of her time and energy into, and started her own business that brings her more peace, joy, freedom, and income.
* She has dates with her husband.
* And my all-time favorite, she takes uninterrupted time to spend with herself, and no, I'm not just talking about showers and sleeping time. She takes legit time away from everything and everyone to check in with herself. Now, that's some real healing and love making!!

When a woman has strong self-validation, she knows her worth and is confident in her choices. She will go shopping alone or with others, and will buy the outfit that she loves without needing her shopping buddies to confirm if she should buy it or not. She is successful in her career, and she knows this without needing the validation of receiving awards, shoutouts, or social media acknowledgements. She knows who she is in her relationships with friends, family, and intimate partners without them constantly having to tell her who she is or where she stands in relationships. She recognizes her insecurities, and will find healthy ways to grow through them, and not put the ownership of being "fixed" onto others. There is also the inner-knowing that you can have feelings without shaming or judging them.

Statements that a woman who has strong self-validation may say:

* The time and commitment I put into my work is connected to my values and beliefs, and not the awards and accolades from others.
* I did an amazing job at work today!
* The dinner I made for my family last night was definitely one of my best, because I felt good about it.
* I accept that I did not feel good about the conversation I had, and I'm not judging myself for it.
* That break I took from social media was so refreshing, and not one time did I think about what others would think about me being away from it.
* My intuition guided me to say no to them, and I'm so glad I listened.
* It makes sense to me why I chose that option, and it's OK if you disagree.

Sometimes the need for outside validation is so strong that we will sometimes ignore what our intuition (or what you may call "gut feeling," but for simplicity we will refer to as intuition in this book) is trying to tell us or show us. Our intuition is there to guide us, help us, and support us. When we stop comparing ourselves, judging ourselves and blaming ourselves, we can start celebrating ourselves. Doesn't that sound so much better? Uhhh, yeah!

Let's get back to Ashley to see what changed the most for her when she started celebrating herself, and not feeling the need to have anyone else's praise.

The biggest changes Ashley felt internally:

* I now get referred to as Zen, which is entertaining and fun to hear.
* I used to be anxious and now I have anxious thoughts I can control. I have a new perspective on what anxiety is.
* I'm chill. I don't fight or fuss as much.
* I'm learning to think before I react, whereas I would react before thinking.
* I can reflect on how others' behaviors are affecting me, and what that means for me.
* The biggest change is that I used to work all of the time to make money, and now I know what is meant for me will find me. I just need to take actionable steps and it will come.

The biggest changes Ashley noticed externally:

* I used to work from sunup to sundown. Now I have a more flowing schedule that aligns with my priorities
* I am present for my children, and can take them to their activities and have random moments of fun with them.
* The words that come out of my mouth are thought out, instead of reactive.
* I now have healthy friendships.
* I make room for friends and connections, whereas before, I didn't have time for lunch or even a phone call.
* I can stop and be with my children and put work aside when they need me.
* It's safe to say I am a lot different overall.
* My husband and I have conversations, whereas before it seemed like arguments. We now come to understandings.
* My presence wears off on other people, and I had to take own-

ership of how I show up around others. People respond to me differently because I'm different.

* Less frustration. Less push and more flow.

I know Ashley doesn't need or want my praise, but I give it to her anyway. HA! This is a real person, not someone from a made-up movie with a sail-off-into-the-sunset type of ending. So, that means you can do this too. We are all real people, searching for real solutions to our challenges. It doesn't have to be the most difficult thing in the world for you; however, it will take you doing things you may not be used to. The payoff is worth it!

A LOVING R.A.W. MESSAGE FROM ASHLEY TO YOU:

Your energy is creating your environment. If you put your energy into positive things, positive things will come out of it. Learn that boundaries don't mean, "I don't love you." They mean, "I love me too." This is not an easy path to travel, but it's worth it. One day you will wake up and realize you are not who you were, and that feels good. There is always internal work to be done. The external work doesn't matter as much as you think it does. What is meant for you will find you if and when you are ready for it. You have to trust yourself even when you don't know how to. Repetition creates habit. Give yourself some F-ing grace! Life can be fun, and life should be fun. Fun doesn't just mean making money. You don't always need to be on guard. Go out and live your life!

SELFIE TIME!

Here are a few fun action steps that can help you on your self-validation journey.

Write down three ideas, dreams, decisions, or changes you want to have right now in your life, but have not felt 100 percent confident making changes for on your own.

_____

_____

_____

_____

_____

_____

_____

_____

_____

_____

_____

_____

_____

_____

What is it about those three things that bring you joy, and how will they impact your life when they actually happen?

_____

_____

_____

_____

_____

_____

_____

_____

_____

_____

_____

_____

_____

_____

_____

_____

_____

_____

_____

Write down one realistic action you will take to bring each of those three desires to life from Step 1.

_____

_____

_____

_____

Fill in the blanks:

I am proud of myself when _____

_____ .

I recognize that I am strong enough to _____

_____ .

The commitment I am making to myself is to _____

_____ .

Now, repeat this statement three times right now out loud. (Or in your mind if you're in a place where speaking out loud is not allowed—also see how I rhymed right there? Lol.)

MY FEELINGS, BELIEFS, AND DESIRES ARE VALID TO ME, AND THAT IS WHAT MATTERS MOST.

KATRINA RAZNIEWSKI'S SELF-VALIDATION STORY

BOXING HERSELF OUT OF CO-DEPENDENCY AND INTO HAPPINESS

Here is the journey of a woman who went from being codependent to rediscovering what happiness meant to her and taking ownership of her life.

About four months after my daughter was born, my post-partum became really bad. I didn't want to leave my house much, and I was with my newborn and my two-year-old son all of the time. When my daughter was born, I was committing most of myself to my kids, my marriage, to my business, and nothing else. My husband worked for the railroad, and being a railroad wife was very challenging for me. I knew it was going to be hard, but I didn't know how hard it really was until my husband wasn't working for them anymore. Even though I had my own career I felt like so much of my identity was wrapped up in the role as a railroad wife, with all that was required of me as being that title.

Going into my marriage, I knew my husband would be on the road a lot and wouldn't be home most nights, so I knew I would be the primary caregiver for our children. With that role being so significant in my life, it didn't allow time for me to do more for myself. You can say being a mom does that in general; however, the difference in what I needed as a wife who was under a bit more strain was that I needed to ask for more help and know that was OK. I wasn't comfortable asking for the help that I needed to make the time for myself. Just being wrapped up in the role of being a mom can be so consuming that you don't see the free time to do it. I felt it was in my nature to put myself last.

The reason I kind of slipped into being this way with doing so much for my kids and not for myself was my co-dependency, which was something I learned about during therapy. When I looked more into that I realized that I was doing that more so with my children. Working through and healing my co-dependency has helped me with knowing that doing things for myself is a necessity, whereas before it felt wrong to put myself first, but I know it's necessary for my own growth. For so long I felt I had to put others before me, but taking time to love me is so important for my healing. I didn't want to be wrapped up in any of my roles so much that I lost myself. It's hard when your identity is wrapped up in one of your roles so much.

I didn't recognize how this was all truly affecting me until I went to my first R.A.W. retreat, and Denise asked who I am outside of my roles. The reason her question hit me so hard was because when my husband lost his job, I was no longer a railroad wife—so what was I? I realized during the retreat that I didn't have many hobbies and didn't know what my current interests were at that time in my life. So, I decided to start jumping into something just for myself. I wanted to figure out what else I enjoyed outside of my kids. I had to give myself permission to explore those things, because

I felt like I was taking time away from my husband, kids, and business. I had to give myself permission to make time for things just for me that weren't about making money, and that weren't for my family. It was frustrating in the beginning, such as days I would want to go to the gym, and I knew I had to figure out what my kids would do while I worked out. In times like that, I felt that my roles were standing in my way, but I still continued to find new ways to make myself a priority. Not exploring my own interests sooner made me more confused about what I wanted out of my life, and I was done with allowing that to hold me back a bit. I was done not using some of my time on myself.

I started boxing again, which was the first step to getting back to myself. I had worked out before in the past, but it felt different this time. When we were struggling financially, I stopped doing things for myself that cost money, like dying my hair and getting my nails done, and I started losing confidence in myself and how I felt about myself. I also started to feel like I was fading into the background, so working out was something that felt good for me. I was so committed to getting healthier that by using that time to focus on myself, I ended up dropping forty pounds. This got me even more excited to do more things for myself. I decided to make a list of things I used to enjoy doing, and decided to go down the list to see if I still enjoyed them, such as doing puzzles, bowling, and playing tennis. By doing more things for myself, I became energized to go out with friends and reconnect with them. Making new friends gave me a better grasp of what my interests were and who I wanted to surround myself with. That in itself has been really good for me.

What has changed for me the most since learning how to validate myself and continue my self-love journey:

Since going through my self-love journey I feel surer of who I am, what I want, what's important to me, and the kind of mom that I want to be. My mom has always been a super mom, and she doesn't take enough time for herself. So, it was hard for me to feel like I could be a super mom if I wasn't exactly the same as my mom is. Now, my confidence has increased in who I am, and what I bring as a mom. I know that I can take time for myself, and that doesn't take away from the type of mom I am for my kids. My confidence now has me owning the type of mom I choose to be without comparison, and that feels so good. My kids see that I have hobbies and make healthy choices for myself, and this will have a lasting positive influence on them as they go through life exploring their own hobbies and taking time to make healthy choices for themselves. My self-love journey hasn't just affected me, it has affected those I love, and to me that is so worth it!

A LOVING R.A.W. MESSAGE FROM KATRINA TO YOU:

Embrace your childlike nature, and think about what a really fun life sounds like to you. Don't say you don't have time, or don't have the money, or you're not good enough at something. Think about some of the things that can bring some fun into your life. If you're struggling to take the time for yourself, then take small steps, because it can be overwhelming when women don't have babysitters, or help, and I know that there are women who don't know how. You may hear people say that it's important to take time for yourself, and you're wondering how. That was me. I had to take responsibility for finding out how, and so do you. I wasn't really having any fun, and that affected me in more ways than I realized. I wasn't dancing, or going on dates with my husband, or doing any fun self-care. Thankfully, I was having fun with my career, but some people don't have that. It's a rough life when you're not having fun, so if nothing else, get a hobby!

CHAPTER THREE

SELF-CONFIDENCE

CAN I DO THIS ON MY OWN?

DEFINITION

Merriam-Webster Dictionary defines self-confidence as, "Confidence in oneself and in one's powers and abilities."

The Counseling Center at University of South Florida had this to say about self-confidence:

Self-confidence is an attitude about your skills and abilities. It means you accept and trust yourself and have a sense of control in your life. You know your strengths and weaknesses well, and have a positive view of yourself. You set realistic expectations and goals, communicate assertively, and can handle criticism.

On the other hand, low self-confidence might make you feel full of self-doubt, be passive or submissive, or have difficulty trusting others. You may feel inferior, unloved, or be sensitive to criticism. Feeling confident in yourself might depend on the situation. For instance, you can feel very confident in some areas, such as academics, but lack confidence in others, like relationships.

Having high or low self-confidence is rarely related to your actual abilities, and mostly based on your perceptions. Perceptions are the way you think about yourself and these thoughts can be flawed.

Low self-confidence might stem from different experiences, such as growing up in an unsupportive and critical environment, being separated from your friends or family for the first time, judging yourself too harshly, or being afraid of failure. People with low self-confidence often have errors in their thinking.

We can all agree that we have each experienced a time or few when we lacked confidence in one or more areas in our lives. The great news is, we are blessed with tools, resources, and various types of support to help us with our self-confidence. It is up to us to seek them out and use them, but it's also true that some people don't feel confident enough to believe the tools, resources, or support will actually help them.

t's story time, and this one is about the journey of a woman who struggled with her confidence, worth, image and so many other SELFIES from a young age that followed her into adult years. This is Ruth's story.

I grew up in a household with an alcoholic father. I loved him, but he used manipulation tactics raising me. He was emotionally abusive, and nothing I did was ever good enough. I remember the turning point of truly not feeling good enough. In eighth grade I brought home a C for pre-algebra. It was the first time I brought home a C. He threw the report card in my face and asked why I didn't receive an A. That's when I started to feel I had to do my best, or it wasn't good enough. I couldn't be proud of myself if he wasn't happy with me. I did everything I thought I was supposed to do. I started college while I was in high school. Graduated as a nurse at the age of twenty. Bought my first house not too long later. I rushed into a marriage with someone that resembled my father's characteristics. Got pregnant on the honeymoon, which I didn't think would happen. I thought it would take me a while to get pregnant, but I also wanted to rush life. I felt I had to rush everything, like I didn't have enough time. My husband and I didn't have a lot of time together with just the two of us before our baby was born. I was a nurse, and he was working the night shift. By the time we had our daughter I remember us arguing a lot, and life was happening fast for us.

After a couple of years, my husband started drinking pretty

heavily. He was always a drinker, but nothing too serious before. I found out he was drinking when he woke up and when he went to bed. I thought it was normal because I saw my dad do the same thing. This went on for years. A few years after our first daughter was born, we had our second daughter. We were both still working a lot, and our marriage wasn't getting any better. When our daughters were two and five years old, I started working for a new company while still working forty to forty-five hours a week as a nurse. My husband was against me working for this new company, and told me I would fail. I still did it, because I needed something to get me out of the house and help me feel like me again. I ended up working more hours between both jobs, and life became monotonous. I had a one-hour commute to and from work, and I didn't see my girls a lot during the week. I was stressed and burning both ends of my candle.

By 2016, I had matched my nursing income with my side business, which had turned out to be much more than a "side gig." Since I was doing well enough with the company, I decided to quit my nursing career, which I felt would make things better at home. This really upset my husband, and his drinking got worse. With him drinking more, our arguing increased as well as the emotional abuse. He started taking Adderall and that made things worse, which was causing so much stress on me and our marriage. He was constantly on a high from the Adderall or a low from the alcohol. I never knew what version of him I would come home to after work, or what the house would look like. It got to the point where I didn't know if I could trust him taking care of our girls. One night our neighbors called me to tell me he left our house with the girls alone while I was working that night. I knew then and there it was past time to make a change. I ended up filing for a divorce in 2018, and hired a private investigator to prove my kids were being left alone and that he was habitually drinking. There was footage of him leaving my kids in the car for thirty minutes while he went to buy alcohol, as well as many instances of him picking up alcohol on the way from work.

During that time, I was struggling with my self-worth and my self-confidence. If I left him, could I do this as a single mom? Would anyone ever want to be with me again? Would I ever find love for myself? I didn't know the answers to those questions, but it didn't matter because I made up my mind that I was leaving him. During that time, I met someone who made me feel alive again. I stepped out of my marriage and had an affair. When the divorce papers were served to my husband, he begged me to stay and said that he would change. He said to please not ruin our family and break up our home, and that our girls need us together. I decided to give him another chance, but I knew I had to be honest with him. I told him about the affair, because I couldn't make a new start with him with lies. I told him that I justified it being OK to have an affair, because I had made up my mind to leave him. He told me we would get through it. I decided to stop the divorce process and try to make things work. Things looked up for about three months, and then shortly after became the worst year of our marriage.

We both agreed to go to counseling, but before we went,

he decided he didn't want us to go. I found out later that he had recorded me admitting to having an affair the day that I told him, and started using it against me. He started taking more Adderall and having hallucinations. The emotional abuse got worse, and I remember being on the floor begging for his forgiveness. He called me a whore, disgusting, and so many other horrible names. I couldn't even forgive myself because he kept throwing the affair back in my face. It happened over and over again almost every day, and then there would be days it felt like a honeymoon, but that never lasted. I couldn't tell anyone because I was ashamed of what I did. Even though I knew I only cheated because I knew my marriage was over. I had never been unfaithful before, but I still couldn't get past it. I tried to forgive myself, but I just couldn't. He would wake me up in the middle of the night telling me my boyfriend was driving down the road during times he was hallucinating. One night I tried to be intimate with him, and I realized he was sweating profusely. I asked him if he could get cleaned up, and he yelled at me that I didn't think it was nasty to be with someone else, so I shouldn't think he was nasty for being sweaty. He continued yelling at me for forty-five minutes that night. I went upstairs to sleep in another room, and I asked God for an answer about what I needed to do. My husband came upstairs banging on the locked door. He told me if I didn't open the door, he would tell our daughters what I did, and that their mother was a slut. I opened the door and told him there is no way he loved me, and to bring our eleven-year-old daughter into this was horrible. I told him to leave me alone or I would call the cops. I closed the door in his face. He texted me ten minutes later asking me to come downstairs, and said that he loved me and didn't mean what he said. I didn't respond. Next morning, he texted me that he was leaving for work, and that he loved me and hoped I had forgiven him. That was the day I called a lawyer to start the divorce process. My mom lived her life like that for so long, and I refused to live my life like that. So, I did what I had to do, and filed for divorce again.

I found out I was pregnant the week after I sought counsel. I was devastated to say the least. Not because I was going to have a baby, but the circumstances surrounding it. I remember sitting on the bathroom floor on Halloween in CVS telling my mama I wanted to die. I couldn't tell anyone about it including my husband at the time because I had already made up my mind to leave my marriage, and I knew he'd use the pregnancy to convince me to stay again. I dried my tears and went home to take my girls trick or treating. I thought at the time that it was the worst day of my life. I didn't know how I would get through it. I had so many confused thoughts going on non-stop. Was God telling me by being pregnant I was to stay in my marriage? Did he want me to try to "fix" it again? Should I stay in this toxic environment with a man who was mistreating me?

The next weekend I spent time with some of my closest friends, and they helped me process the turmoil I was going through. We made plans knowing that I'd have a baby in July, and I started accepting the fact that I would be a single mom to a newborn. I even got excited about buying baby clothes and having a new born baby in my arms again.

On November 10, early in the morning, I started bleeding. I was so scared and I had no idea what was happening. I had a big team meeting that day, and I couldn't bring myself to go to the ER because I realized what was happening. I was losing my little angel. My leadership team stepped in and helped me run my meeting that day. The next day I spent eight hours in the emergency room alone confirming that I had in fact had a miscarriage. My husband never even knew I was pregnant, and honestly it wouldn't have changed anything had he known.

During that time a lot happened. He dodged papers several times. There were even occasions when the authorities tried serving him, and he would stand in the doorway wearing scary masks, laughing. On our daughter's eighth birthday, our daughters found out about us getting a divorce. My oldest daughter asked me what was wrong on that day, and I told her everything was OK. Their dad told me to tell them the truth about how I was breaking up our family. That was not the day or the way I wanted our girls to find out what was going on. Things escalated quickly. He refused to leave the house, so I had to move out. I stayed with my mom, with friends, and pretty much lived out of my car for a couple of months. I was accused of horrible things during that time. I knew going through a divorce was not going to be easy, but it was ten times harder than I ever imagined it would be. We worked out an agreement where we would live in the house at separate times, so the girls' lives wouldn't be disrupted. A couple of times he refused to leave during the times I was scheduled to stay at the house, so I had to take legal action to get him to cooperate. While at the court hearing he had to take a drug test, which he failed, so I was awarded full custody until he had a clean drug test. Months went by when he couldn't see the kids, and our girls blamed me because he told them I wouldn't let them see him. My girls and I struggled a lot during that time. There was so much fighting between me and their dad, and it was causing a major strain on our entire family. Whenever he had time to see the kids and I had time to myself, I tried finding ways to get myself better emotionally and mentally. Believe it or not, that was almost as hard as going through the divorce, because I had never taken the time to find out what I needed. It was always about pleasing others, to prove that I was good enough. Well, now it was time for me to take care of myself, and I just had to figure out how!

Ruth went through years of absolute hell, and sometimes when you are living in your own version of hell, it feels as though you will never get out of it. Someone reading this may have been triggered reading about one or more parts of Ruth's story: her divorce; making up only to separate again; the verbal, mental, and emotional abuse from her father and husband; getting pregnant at a point that she felt was not the best time; having a miscarriage; having her children resent her because of the lies her husband was telling them about her; feeling lost and confused and wanting to die because that seemed to be the only way out. This is a real story with real raw feelings, consequences, and fears. Ruth had to live through this, and so many women have lived a very similar life as she did. Ruth realized her self-confidence and self-worth challenges started from childhood, and from someone who was meant to protect and love her. That feeling of not being good enough played front and center in so many parts of her life. We cannot be quick to judge someone on their situation, because for one—who are we to judge? And two—you don't always know someone's story.

How are YOU feeling right now? Has your heart rate quickened, or your breathing changed from its usual pace? Whether they have or have not, let's all take a few deep cleansing breaths. Taking a few moments throughout the day to bring awareness to our breathing helps to ease our mind, our heart rate, and our nerves. Reading Ruth's story was a lot to take in, and I want to make sure you are okay. Please take one minute to jot down a few thoughts you're having before you continue to read, even if you feel you're doing fine right now. You may be surprised at what comes up for you.

_____

_____

_____

_____

_____

_____

_____

_____

_____

Thank you for taking a few moments to check in on yourself. It is so important to make a habit of doing so.

Now, let's get back to it!

When a woman is not feeling strong in her self-confidence, she may say statements such as:

* I'm not strong enough to do this.
* Maybe if I change the way I act she/he/they will finally accept me.
* I'm afraid I can't do this on my own.
* I look better than her/him/them, so why do they get everything and I don't?
* I left the conversation wondering what others thought about me.
* I'm getting older, and it's probably too late to get what I really want out of my life.
* It's their fault I can't _____ .
* I'm just not good enough.
* There's nothing I can do about it, so I'm giving up.
* I've tried doing _____ so many times, and I just can't get it right. What's wrong with me?
* I know I want to _____, but I have no motivation.

Self-confidence is one of those SELFIES that you can feel good about in some areas, and feel absolutely on the lower end in other areas. You may have strong self-confidence in your career, and feel low self-confidence as a caregiver. You may feel like the most confident person on earth when it comes to your physical health, but have low self-confidence when it comes to how you view yourself in relationships with others. This scenario can work in various areas in your life, and sometimes when we lack self-confidence, we can deflect and become judgmental toward others.

Confidence can also flourish or diminish based on who you surround yourself with. You have probably heard the saying that you are the company you keep. Having friends, family members, a coach who specializes in what you are hoping to increase in your life, guidance of some sort, and a strong and supportive cheerleading squad are all so beneficial to increasing your confidence, and how you view your life. That's why I feel confident telling my clients just working with me and/or attending one of my retreats will raise the levels on their SELFIE meter, because I strive to provide the space, guidance, and attention to each client to help them on their Self-Love journey. One of my clients told me that attending my R.A.W. retreats is like fresh oxygen for her. This particular woman and many others in our community are able to gain clarity on who they truly are and how they want to live their own lives based on their vision and goals, not based on what others are telling them to do or how they are supposed to live. This not only helps the women with their overall health, it also helps them to strengthen the relationships they value in their lives, find new interests and hobbies that bring them joy, let go of the relationships that are no longer for them, increase their income in their jobs/careers/businesses, leave jobs that are no longer for them, start new careers or businesses that make their hearts sing with joy, and heal in ways they did not know were possible. Another benefit for the women who are mothers is that they are able to see their child(ren) for who they really are, and not as younger humans who need to live out their parents' dreams.

One of my clients not only learned new ways to value her own time outside of being a mom and a wife. She started having different conversations with her children by getting to truly know their desires, dreams, fears, questions about life, and how she can support them without always coming from a place of, "I know best, because I'm your mom." What if moms started seeing their children as humans who are having their own life experience, and not people who are here to live out the dreams they want for them, marry the person they want for them, have the career they want for them or even believe in the same religion that they believe in. What if moms (dads too, but I'm speaking to women, so...) supported and loved their children from a place of wanting to help their children flourish in their own light, and not the light they feel their child needs to flourish in? How much happier would children be? How much happier would moms be? How much stronger would the mother-and-child relationship become? We create confidence in our children by being confident in ourselves and being confident that we may not always know what's best but we are willing to learn, listen, and understand.

When a woman has low self-confidence, it resembles some of the ways Ruth felt:

* If I excel in school, my parents will be proud of me.
* If I work hard and make a name for myself, then I will finally prove I'm worthy of something.

* I can't leave him, because I don't know if I can raise my children on my own.

* I messed up in our relationship, so maybe I deserve being called ugly names.

* It's okay for my husband to drink a lot, because my dad did it and my mom lived with him doing so.

* I have to try harder because what I'm doing right now is not good enough. I can never please (insert person here).

* I can never seem to do anything right for my children.

* I will only go to the gym when hardly anyone is there because I don't want people staring at me.

* My anxiety is at an all-time high when I have to talk in front of a group of people, because I may mess up or forget something.

Ruth is not the first or the last woman to have these thoughts, and to live through what she did. Ruth is just like someone reading this book, but remember, just because the story is similar, the ending of that chapter will look different. Your situation changes from bad to worse, or from bad to better depending on what you are willing to do to change your situation. IT IS NOT EASY! However, this is where I'm going to throw in that quote from Matt Hogan, "Choose Your Hard!" and give you three seconds right now to decide which HARD you are choosing. Work? Your health? Your relationship? Your children? Whether to relocate or not? Or something else? Life will not always be easy, because we will have moments of HARD, but we can choose our HARD, so choose wisely.

What HARD are you choosing right now?

_____

_____

_____

_____

_____

_____

For some women who struggle with low self-confidence, it stems from childhood. You may notice a pattern with most of the chapters in this book, that a lot of our challenges do start from our younger years. This applies for those who had the absolute worst childhoods imaginable, those who had the most loving childhoods that resembled fairy tales, and every other scenario in between. It doesn't even always have to do with those who raised us in our households; it could be someone at your church, your school, the friends you had, music teachers, sports coaches, the children or adults you encountered at various events. One significant moment, or many significant moments can play a major role in the way we see ourselves and how we live our lives.

I started playing the violin at the age of six, and I learned to play by ear. For those who may not be familiar with what that means, I learned how to play the violin by listening to music and not reading music. I had to get familiar with the different sounds that came from each string, and each finger placement. So, when I would hear a song I could pick up where to place my fingers, and on which string. My mother and grandmother would play records for me or sing songs and that's how I learned. I even came up with my own way of writing my notes, which was not the way you would learn with a professional instructor, but it worked for me. I would perform for various church events that would sometimes have thousands of people in the audience. I felt confident as a violinist. Then one day I started working with a classical music instructor and had to learn a completely new way of reading music and playing my violin. I felt like a failure every time I would go to my private lessons and our Saturday group lessons. What came so easy to me before now seemed wrong, and I was embarrassed. I didn't feel as though I was as good as the other students, and I felt I was constantly letting my instructor down. I started to shy away from performing for church events and would say that I was too sick to go to my lessons, because I felt that I wasn't good enough to play. Where I once felt so confident, and would dream of performing at Carnegie Hall, I now felt like my musical skills were not even close to being good enough for anything. I continued to play over the years, but my confidence took such a hit that I stopped dreaming about performing for Carnegie Hall and just accepted the fact that I was just an OK violinist. I thought I would be better suited to teach others how to play, and that's what I did for several years. I eventually stopped teaching and performing altogether, and I didn't pick up my violin for years. This need to either be the best or not do it at all trickled over into other areas of my life, and it wasn't until my thirties that I started to really see that this was a big issue that I needed to rectify. I got to a point of saying, "This cannot be how I live my life," so I decided to make some changes. I started getting professional support in a life coach, paying attention to how I felt around certain people to see if those relationships needed to change, found a new therapist to help me heal in different areas of my life, learned techniques to forgive situations from my past, put more focus into my spiritual well-being, and I implemented new morning practices such as listening to uplifting Audibles and podcasts, increasing my gratitude, and even changing how I saw my physical health. Through those changes my confidence increased and I no longer have that "perfectionist" mentality. Now, I play the violin for myself and my fur babies, but only because I don't have the desire to perform on stage. However, I do have some fun news! In 2021, I bought a cello and eventually found an instructor to teach me how to play it. This was a big deal for me. For years I wanted to learn how to play the cello, but because my confidence was in the dumps, I thought it would be a waste of time. Well, one day I decided I wanted to learn a new hobby, and I revisited some long-lost dreams of mine and landed on wanting to learn the cello. That same day I went to the music store, tested out a few cellos, and purchased one. I did not waste any time. I am confident that I will continue having fun learning how to play the cello, and I don't have any future plans for it. Sometimes being confident is doing something just because you want to without any agenda for it.

By now you have probably figured out that this book isn't just for you to graze through and toss it to the side and forget about it. This book is to help you whether in a teeny tiny way, a "that was cool" way, or "this straight up changed my life" way. We are given tools, resources, love, appreciation, whispers and loud shouts of encouragement and guidance in so many different ways. Allow this book to be something useful for you. Some of the ways you can have this book work in your favor is to take your time reading each chapter without distractions, participate in the activities even if you feel they don't apply to you right now in your life, let your ego take a break and lower your defenses as you read something that may trigger you **(remember, it's not realistic to be perfect, and we all have "stuff" we can work on)**, and be open to what may come to you as a gentle loving ray of hope from each story, example, or paragraph. This book is also to help you with your "What Ifs..." I want to encourage you to stay open to how this book may help you, and you might just notice how your moods start to shift in your more challenging relationships, how your mindset shifts on yourself and your life, or how the spectrum for one or more of your SELFIES increase. Now, let's get back to Ruth.

What if Ruth decided to stay with her husband and not file for divorce? We can safely say that her girls would have been a part of a similar cycle Ruth was a part of when she was a young girl, when she watched what her mother endured from her father. Ruth didn't want that for her girls, and she didn't want that for herself. She knew she needed to make some humongous changes, and she was willing to do what it took. You only read a part of Ruth's story, and none of us can actually know everything she went through. Even with the little we know about Ruth, we know leaving her husband was the best option; however, we also know that when we are conditioned a certain way for years to believe something about ourselves, it is a tough shell to crack. Ruth had to figure out how to increase her confidence, change her beliefs about her worth, truly love herself for who she is, and start a new chapter for her and her girls when so much of her past made her feel that it was all impossible.

Let's see what happened to Ruth after she moved out of her house.

I started reading my Bible more and having devotion time every morning. Reading, journaling, and going to the gym for an hour a day became my daily routine. Even with my new routine I knew I still needed some additional support, and guess what? I found it! I ended up seeing a post one day for one spot left for a mindset transformation retreat for women, and I felt it was a message from God that I needed to be there. I booked it without knowing how much it would cost. The retreat was a couple of weeks away, and I knew my girls would be taken care of while I was gone, but I didn't know who would take care of my pets. I knew I would find a way because I had to attend that retreat. I have never traveled alone, and I was scared. I was nervous because I didn't know what to expect. I didn't know who would be there, but I knew I had to do it.

One day during the retreat we had a beach day, and at one point there were dragonflies everywhere. I looked up in the clouds as I was talking to Denise, and I saw angel wings. The reason this was meaningful for me was because the day my dad died in 2014, there were dragonflies everywhere. That moment sitting on the beach with Denise having a deep conversation about what I was going through, and seeing the dragonflies and angel wings in the clouds, was the first time in a long time I felt peace. I wanted to let go of not being good enough and feeling like I was not good enough for anyone. The rest of the retreat was liberating. I remember leaving with a sense of hope. I felt freedom, peace, and that everything would be OK. I ended up hiring Denise as my private coach to work on my mindset, and I worked with her weekly for several months. She gave me assignments, and one of the most impactful assignments was taking myself out on a date. This may seem simple to some, but trust me, we had a lot of work to do before we got to that date assignment. I went to the Melting Pot for my solo date, and took my journal and my Bible. I journaled, ate, and read. I realized at dinner I never went out to eat by myself, and I also never went on a trip by myself. So, I reached out to a friend who owns a cabin, and she offered it to me at no charge. I was alone with my journal and my Bible. On one of our coaching calls, Denise asked me what the scariest reality for me was, and I said being alone. She asked me why I didn't like being alone. I told her because it was too quiet. She asked if it was too quiet or too loud. I realized it was too loud. So, on that cabin trip alone I spent time reflecting on that conversation, and I continued to journal and read my Bible. I thought about what type of husband I want in my future. I made a list and I prayed about it.

When I got home from my solo trip, I started dating, and found a lot of hurtful people. I found out that there are a lot of narcissists in the world, and people who want to use you and not care about your wellbeing. I started figuring out warning signs for if someone was worth having a relationship with me or not. There was one person in particular that had me fooled for a period of time, and he made me believe that he was everything I wanted in a man. He was a liar and a manipulator. Looking back, I believe God placed those people in my life for me to see who was meant for me, and who was not meant for me. Those experiences showed me how I deserved to be treated and not be treated. It took a lot of work, but I eventually got to a place of truly loving myself, and peace in knowing I didn't need anyone to complete me. Then, one day after deciding I was done with dating for a long time and that I was OK being alone and raising my daughters, I randomly received a message from someone asking if I would go on a date with him. He saw things in me that he wanted to get to know better. I told him I was having a difficult time trusting men, so I was being cautious about stepping into something new. Something inside me told me to go for it, and two days later we went on a date.

Before the date we talked a lot about so many things. For our first date, we went out for lunch, which then turned to dinner, and I remember being so nervous because he seemed like the type of man I had prayed for. That day I knew he was the man I was going to marry. It wasn't a feeling of desperation or wanting someone to fill a void. At that point in my life, I was feeling so much more confident within myself, and I knew that I was worthy of honest and pure love. I had to first learn how to give myself the love I was wanting from someone else and come to an understanding that I am worthy and more than enough. For so long I didn't know if I could fully trust my instincts, because they had failed me many times before, but this time it felt different and it was because I was different. After dinner we went out for ice-cream because we didn't want the date to end. When we left the restaurant, he opened my door for me and buckled my seatbelt. I thought, "Wow, no one has buckled my seatbelt for me before." I felt safe with him already, and not just because of the seatbelt. It was just a feeling that I completely trusted. After getting ice-cream while sitting in the car, he kissed me.

I remember getting home thinking how amazing he was. He texted me that night after dropping me off to tell me he missed me. I ended up seeing him again the next day and then the next day. We had coffee one day and talked for so long, and I knew I could talk to him forever. When I got in the car after our coffee date, I turned on the radio before pulling off, and a beautiful song was playing. He grabbed my hand and I got out of the car, and we danced in the Starbucks parking lot. The next song that came on was one of my daddy's favorite songs, and I felt that was a sign from my daddy that this man was the one. I felt so special, and so happy.

Life started happening at full speed after that. I had a business trip to go on, and I missed him so much. I came home to sticky notes all over my house from him, saying how much he missed me. He told me there were five notes, but I only found four. I couldn't find the fifth one. He eventually told me that there wasn't a fifth note, and that he just told me that to keep me on my toes, because he wanted me to know that he was always thinking of me. I had another business trip six weeks after meeting him, and I came home to more sticky notes all over the house again. The notes described everything he loved about me. Then there was one on the bathroom mirror asking me to marry him. There was a "Yes," "No," and, "Maybe," and it was signed, "Love, Your Husband." Of course, I said yes. When we talked about dates, I asked him if we could get married on my daddy's birthday which is September 17, but that date wasn't available. So, we decided to get married on September 19, and combine our beautiful families. We have three girls between the two of us, and the night of the wedding we got pregnant. Not too long later we ended up losing our baby, which was hard emotionally. I was so excited about being pregnant, and it was taken away. We decided not to do any ovulation testing and let God take over. Not too long after, I became pregnant again, and now we are expecting our baby girl in July. We are so excited for the growth of our family. During that whole experience looking back, I know I had to go through the trials and tribulations to be the woman that I am for myself, my daughters, and my husband. There were times in my darkest days that I didn't want to wake up. It was a hard journey learning my worth, and how I deserve to be treated. I am God's child and God's children aren't meant to be abused.

I just have to say that the women who are sharing their stories in this book are incredible women, and I love them all so much. It has been a joy to watch their transformations, and see them take control over how they show up in their lives. This was not an overnight process for Ruth as you read. This was a long journey, and thankfully she made the necessary changes so the rest of her life can be lived in love, joy, respect, fun, and her favorite word—peace.

When a woman has strong self-confidence, she makes statements such as:

* I'm choosing the HARD that will benefit me, because any other way is not acceptable.
* My life is worth fighting for, and I may not have all of the answers, but I will figure it out.

* I excel in my career because I put the work and energy into it, and not to prove myself but because I enjoy what I do.

* The love I have for myself is much deeper than the love anyone else can give me, and the love they give me will be nothing short of amazing.

* I can do the difficult things, because that's what has to be done.

* I know I'm worthy of peace and joy in my life, and that is what I am available for.

* If you mistreat me then there is no room for you in my life.

* Just because my childhood wasn't the best, doesn't mean the rest of my life has to copycat that.

* I know better, because I do better.

WARNING, WARNING, WARNING!!! I'm about to give you a big hug with my words.

YOU deserve to be confident!

YOU are not the ugly words people may have called you, or you may have called yourself.

YOU have a confidence within you that is begging to be front and center.

YOU know which HARD to choose, because you know it will bring some ease and peace into your life.

YOU are worthy of being confident, standing in your confidence, owning your confidence, and singing "Confident" by Demi Lovato.

I think it's time for a solo dance party (or you can grab your child, your pet or whoever is close by to join in), and no, I do not care if you are at work or sitting in a doctor's waiting room. It's time to dance! Go to YouTube, find Demi's song about confidence, and dance your butt off!

Uh-uh... don't even think about reading the next sentence until you have your dance party!

Now that we have danced a bit and gotten our heart rate up, let's see what Ruth wants to share with us about the biggest changes for her after building up her self-confidence:

* I now have peace! That word got brought up a lot during my coaching with Denise, and I was always searching for it. I never had peace and always had anxiety, and now I have peace.

* People tell me I glow. They can see happiness within me shining through. I'm in a relationship with someone who cherishes me and shows me daily how much he loves and respects me. I have a bonus daughter from my new husband, and a newborn baby on the way.

* I know I am good enough, and I get to be an even better example for all of my girls on what a confident woman looks and feels like!

Ruth, you are not just an example for your daughters, you are a great example for so many people who know you and who are reading about you!

A LOVING R.A.W. MESSAGE FROM RUTH TO YOU:

Life isn't always going to be hard. Find a routine that works. Wake up with gratitude every day. Focus on the things that you can change, and not the things that you can't. And love yourself fully. It takes work, but you're worth it!

SELFIE TIME!

What area(s) do you feel confident in right now in your life?

_____

_____

_____

_____

_____

_____

_____

_____

What area(s) in your life do you want to increase your confidence in right now?

_____

_____

_____

_____

_____

_____

_____

_____

_____

What is one step you will commit to today to start increasing your confidence by 10 percent?

_____

_____

_____

_____

_____

_____

_____

_____

_____

What is one step you will commit to this month to start increasing your confidence by 25 percent?

_____

_____

_____

_____

_____

_____

_____

_____

NAKRISTIN GREENE'S SELF-CONFIDENCE STORY

HOW SHE WENT FROM "LIVING" TO ALIVE!

Here is a story about a woman who went from feeling like she was just "living" to feeling completely ALIVE.

During the darkest time in my life, I didn't feel like I would overcome anything. I thought I was a bad person, and deserved to have bad things happen to me. I felt I was in a deep dark hole with no way out, and that I would never see daylight again. Even though I saw my two kids every day, I truly was just going through the motions of being a mom and taking care of their needs. I really believed I lost my life, even though I was still "living." Some of the thoughts I would have about myself I would never say to anyone else: "I'm horrible." "No one will love me." "I'm not worthy of having a good partner." "I'm a horrible parent, and my kids will hate me." I would use things that happened in my life to validate my negative thoughts. What led to that dark period was one major event that shed light on so many other events leading up to it. One night, my kids' father put a gun to my face, and when that happened it reaffirmed to me that I was in a toxic relationship and the way I was living my life was not OK.

There were constant signs that the relationship I was in was harmful to me and my children. I remember one time my eight-year-old daughter told me if her dad and I would just be nice to each other that we could stay together. My daughter saw us fighting on too many occasions. She saw things in our relationship that were not OK, but I would find excuses and justify those behaviors. The night he put the gun to my face was when I started to snap out of it. I knew if I stayed in that relationship, I may not survive.

Our relationship wasn't always that bad. In the beginning he made me feel like a queen, and once I became pregnant with our daughter, he started to show his true colors. Something in him changed, and the changes happened slowly over time. I believe it was partly connected to the people we were around. We would be around other couples who were always arguing, and even though I tried to stay away from those types of couples, it still seeped into our relationship. Once it started getting bad, it was really bad, and I couldn't leave for so many reasons. That was the only relationship in which I had experienced that type of toxicity.

I asked myself many times what it was about him or the relationship that got me to a place of losing myself, and I couldn't pinpoint it. I wanted to make changes for myself and for my children. I just didn't know how to ask for help, especially when I hit rock bottom.

I understood that not knowing how to get help was not an excuse I could afford, so I had to find ways to feel better about myself before my life became any worse. I started spending time with friends who could relate to me, and who were also working on themselves to become better.

Reading emails from Pastor Joseph Prince every morning was definitely uplifting and gave me hope that my life could and would turn around. I joined the one-year R.A.W. group coaching program led by Denise Marsh, which gave me the tools for my healing journey and helped me learn realistic ways of accepting myself and loving myself. Journaling my thoughts instead of saying them out loud to someone also became a big part of my self-love journey. This was not an overnight process, and I am still a work in progress... but aren't we all? The difference between who I am now and who I was is that I love myself, and I love the life that I am living, and that was not something I was able to say for so long. My children now have a mother who is excited about living, and this is helping them to thrive in more ways than I can count.

Having low self-confidence cost me:

* My womanhood. I lost who I was as a woman. I lost myself in that relationship.

* I used to be so full of energy before the relationship, fun to be around with a goofy side, life of the party, would make friends everywhere I would go, and somewhere along the way in the relationship I lost all of that.

* Living my life fully. I didn't get to hang out with my friends much, because he would make me feel bad about it. It wasn't an issue in the beginning, but it became an issue as time went on.

What has changed for me since being on my self-love journey:

*   My attitude and my perception of people. I used to put people on high pedestals, and then would get disappointed, or pre-judge them to a point that I would not get to know them. Now, I take the time to get to know people, and allow them to show themselves to me.

*   I used to have a really bad attitude—it didn't matter if you were a friend or an enemy, I would curse you out or argue with you over anything. Now I don't give anyone that energy of acting in a negative way—I realize if I react in a negative way it's hurting myself.

*   I used to be quick to react, and not in the best way. I used to not think about consequences or who I would hurt—I would just react if I was hurt. Now l think about the consequences before I react when someone upsets or hurts me.

*   My confidence and self-worth have increased. I am still working on increasing my confidence even more; however, I am so proud to say that I have made tremendous growth.

*   I know I am worthy of real love, and I will not settle for just any person.

*   Thoughts I have now: "One day I will have a loving husband, who will accept me for who I am." "I am not a perfect mother, but I am a great mother." "I have flaws, and I accept myself and work on the parts that need more love."

*   My body has changed. There was a point where I wasn't eating when I was stressed or depressed. When I started removing the toxic mindset, energy, and people, I started to gain healthy weight and eat regularly.

*   I have learned how to forgive. Two people I was able to forgive

were my grandfather and my children's father. Yes, my children's father hurt me in so many ways, but I have since healed and continue to heal from those wounds, and I am no longer carrying around those feelings that kept me feeling like a prisoner in my own mind. My grandfather wasn't a grandfather figure to me, and I resented him for it for so long. Even though he has passed away, I was able to learn healthy ways to forgive him, and understood that the forgiveness was also about freeing the anger and hurt that was inside me.

* My children have benefited from my changes, because I was a very angry mommy before. I used to apologize so often to them, because I would take my anger out on them. Now, because I am calmer and have more control over my emotions, I don't have to apologize as often because I am not taking my anger out on them.

* I have rediscovered what my purpose is in my own life.

* Most importantly, I have rediscovered who I am as a woman.

A R.A.W. LOVING MESSAGE FROM NAKRISTIN TO YOU:

It's possible to love yourself, it just takes time. When you are going through the journey of rediscovering yourself, you have to go through every part of yourself, even the parts you try to hide from. Healing is not an overnight process. It's not easy, but have patience. I'm not the most patient person, so if I can do it, I am here to tell you it is definitely possible for you.

QUICK SELF-LOVE SPECTRUM CHECK-IN

Please take a few moments to re-evaluate where you are on the Self-Love Spectrum. Has it changed since starting this book, now that you may view your Selfies in a different way?

|---------------|---------------|---------------|---------------|---------------|

SELF-LOATHING   SELF-DISLIKE   SELF-COMPLACENCY   SELF-LIKE   SELF-LOVE

_____

_____

_____

_____

_____

CHAPTER FOUR

SELF-IMAGE

WHO WOULD WANT TO SEE THE REAL ME?

DEFINITION

Now, if you're wondering what SELF-IMAGE really means, there are many ways to define it.

Merriam-Webster Dictionary defines it as, "One's conception of oneself or of one's role."

An article I read from the Cleveland Clinic describes it as,

The personal view, or mental picture, that we have of ourselves. Self-image is an "internal dictionary" that describes the characteristics of the self, including such things as intelligent, beautiful, ugly, talented, selfish, and kind. These characteristics form a collective representation of our assets (strengths) and liabilities (weaknesses) as we see them.

To simplify it, self-image is how we see ourselves. I know, I pretty much just summed up what the clinic and Merriam-Webster's Dictionary said. We don't need to complicate this. Let's just get down to it!

et me introduce you to my client, Jaimie Brewis, who struggled with her self-image for years, to the point where it affected most of her relationships, her social life, and her overall confidence. Continue reading to see if any part of Jaimie's story sounds like something you've been through or are currently going through.

My story goes back to high school. My biggest challenge during that time was my weight. In high school, I was bigger than all of the other girls in my grade. I was tall and heavier in weight than everyone. To give you an idea, I was five feet eight inches and 220 pounds. One of my closest friends at the time was five feet two inches and small in weight. Almost everyone I knew played sports, and I just didn't feel like I fit in anywhere. Looking back, I remember the complex I had with not "fitting in" with anyone my age. I was in the drama club, and even there I felt like the odd person out. Not fitting in was a struggle for me since before high school through adulthood, and it's something I feel I had to constantly think about my entire life. My weight was the main reason this was a challenge for me, and it was something I thought about 24/7 through high school, college, and my twenties.

In high school I never wanted to wear ponytails because I thought people would think my face was fat. I wore baggy clothes to try to hide my weight, but those baggy clothes did not hide my insecurities. In college, I decided to start working out, and I dropped weight pretty quickly. I had a new boyfriend, but it was not a good relationship. He would say things to me that weren't OK, and I knew this, but I also didn't leave the relationship right away. I remember one time he texted me telling me he was at a strip club, and a stripper was sitting on his lap. Eventually I left that relationship, but the next relationship wasn't much better. My next boyfriend cheated on me, which left me feeling worse about myself during that time. The similarity in both relationships was that I was disrespected, and I didn't want to believe that was what I deserved.

Looking back, I now know that I had low self-esteem and low self-worth, but I didn't recognize it at the time. Someone showed interest in me, and because of my low self-esteem I would accept the interest, regardless of if they were nice or not. I failed my second year at Michigan State, which wasn't like me because I was always getting good grades. Throughout my education years, I knew I had to get good grades and be a good girl, because I wanted to please my parents, so having to move back home because I failed in college was not helping me with my self-esteem whatsoever. I always felt I had to be perfect, and live up to high expectations for everyone else, and I never took the time to think about what I wanted for myself.

After some time, I decided to change my degree to nursing. I graduated and received my nursing degree, which was a win for me but that was short-lived. Even though I had my nursing degree, I couldn't pass my state boards, and I started getting down on myself again. During this time my mom was going through cancer, my boyfriend was cheating on me, and it was probably the darkest period in my life. I cut people out of my life, because I was so embarrassed about everything I felt I wasn't. I felt like a huge failure. I didn't want to tell my friends and family that I couldn't pass my nursing boards, so I just avoided them altogether so I didn't have to explain anything or listen to their sympathy.

I was twenty-five years old with a body image that I didn't love. Even though I lost weight, I had body dysmorphia. I got down to 160 pounds, but I still thought I was fat. There was never a time I looked in the mirror and thought I looked good. Imagine losing a significant amount of weight, and still not thinking you look good. Isn't losing weight supposed to make us feel beautiful and worthy? Apparently not!

When I say this was the lowest point in my life, it is not an exaggeration. On top of my failures in school, still hating my body, and having to leave a relationship that lowered my self-esteem even more than what it was, I also had a hard time making money. Jeez, I just couldn't catch a break! I was behind on my credit card bills, and at one point my electricity was cut off. I eventually filed for bankruptcy, and I figured my life couldn't get any worse than what it was. My self-esteem was getting lower and lower, and I felt like less than a failure (whatever that is, if that's even a thing). I will say something started to click for me, and there was something inside of me that told me to follow the path that felt right. I really wanted to trust my inner wisdom. I just didn't know how!

Jaimie's story is not that different from someone who is reading this book. She thought shedding pounds would somehow make her feel better about herself. Are you the person who can relate to Jaimie, or is there someone you know who can? Let's talk a bit more about what it's like when a woman has a low self-image.

Statements that a woman may say when she views her self-image in a negative or un-loving way:

* I am not smart enough to apply for that position, even though I think I'll be good at it. My co-worker deserves it more than I do.

* Please don't tell me I look good in this outfit, because I know I don't.

* There is no way I'm taking any pictures this holiday with my family, because I look disgusting.

* Everyone expects me to be bubbly and high energy, but I'm more introverted. What if they don't want to be my friend if I start acting like the real me?

* It must be my lucky day, because there is no way I could have pulled off that project without luck on my side.

* When I was a child, I always felt like I was in the background, and I find myself still feeling like I'm in the background in one or more areas in my life. No one ever notices me.

* Who would want to have sex with me looking like this? I don't even want to look at myself with clothes on in the mirror, so being naked in front of anyone is a no go!

* If I wear these baggy clothes, maybe people won't notice that I've gained weight.

* Of course, I can't find love. My own mother/father never loved me, so why would anyone else?

* I wish I had my face on her/his/their body, then I would look amazing!

* If I start telling people I'm starting my own business, will they think I'm stupid for even trying? Ugh, who am I kidding, I'm not doing it.

When a woman is not confident in her self-image, she:

* Misses out on taking pictures of herself with loved ones on special occasions, family trips, outings with friends, and other beautiful moments, because she is so concerned with the way she looks that she is afraid of judgment, criticism or feeling worse than she already does.

* Feels she never fits in with anyone or any groups, even those she may be interested in.

* Is afraid of meeting new people or being open to new relationships, because she is ashamed, embarrassed and self-conscious of her looks and/or her intelligence level.

* Focuses more on her physical appearance over her mental and emotional health.

* Will get in the wrong relationship with someone who shows her interest, because she feels that may be the best she can do.

* Doesn't go after the job, promotion, or business venture, because she doesn't believe she would actually be great at it or feels she doesn't deserve it.

* Spends money on improving her physical appearance in order to be accepted and/or loved by others.

* Feels her self-worth and self-confidence is determined by the way she looks, the job she has, the amount of money in her bank account, or the number of degrees and accolades she has received.

Honesty time!

When you were reading the statements above, which ones were true for you? Which statements seemed similar to what you think of yourself or tell yourself most often? Maybe you actually say some of those statements about yourself, or similar statements out loud to people you know. You may even make a joke about your physical appearance or intellect to hide your insecurities. Remember, this is not a shame festival; this is a self-awareness adventure! When I think about the way I used to talk to myself about my body, it would make some of you truly shake your head and want to give me a hug. I was so cruel to myself for so long when it came to my body that you would've thought someone beat me into thinking I was ugly, too thin, too big, or just downright disgusting. There was a time I refused to touch a carb, because I thought they were the darn Devil and would make me big as a house. These were thoughts I had when I was 95 pounds AND when I was 185 pounds!!!! Sooooo, does that confirm that our poor body image doesn't ALWAYS have to do with our weight, it's mostly our mentality. Does this sound like a stage you were once in, or are currently in? I promise, you are not alone, and you also don't have to be a victim to that type of thinking.

Look, I love french fries and I actually deprived myself of those crispy pieces of heaven for years because of what I thought OTHERS would think of me. Jesus, take the dang wheel! Why do we do this to ourselves??? Yes, I do pay attention to what I eat now, but it's a different mentality when it comes to eating for me. I don't count calories or worry about carbs. It's more about what's good for my gut health, my heart health, what's going to give me energy or deplete my energy, what's going to be good for my skin, and what is good for MY body type—not the person I saw on Facebook as I was scrolling my newsfeed.

Temperature Check!
What are you thinking right now? Are you thinking, "HECK YEAH, I am ready to make some changes in the way I see myself!"? Or are you thinking, "Denise, this chapter may help some people, but I've tried and tried to get better about the way I see myself and nothing works for me." Aaaaaaaaahhhhhhh, I get it! Both sides of it. It doesn't matter if you are eighteen years old right now or eighty-nine years old. If you are breathing right now, you can change the way you see yourself if you are willing to change your beliefs about yourself.

Remember, those unloving, unkind, and abusive thoughts you've been having for days or years were put into your belief system by others: people who love you in their own way (insert sigh here); social media filters, social media posts, magazine articles of the rich and famous; one or more of your school teachers who probably shouldn't have been a teacher; bullies (sidenote: bullies can come in all forms—parents, siblings, other family members, mentors, bosses, authority figures, that woman in your book club, and that's the short list); and a few other factors could have contributed to how you see yourself. So, if you believe all of that to be true, then you can also believe that you can choose to create new beliefs for yourself and about yourself.

Still not convinced? Ok then, find the nearest child under five years old, and ask them if they think they are smart, creative, brave, cute, and a future doctor or business owner. Oh wait, some of them may not think that, because they are being raised by bullies! They have already had people bigger than them tell them, "Stop drawing on the walls—you're being bad," instead of redirecting the child to drawing on paper and encouraging their artistic nature without belittling them. Or, they may have already heard someone bigger than them comment on how the child across the street can already count to thirty, and they cannot, so they may start thinking something is wrong with them. What about the child who wanted an afternoon snack, but the person bigger than them told them they can't have it because they will get fat like Aunt Mildred? Kids are bullied, because the adults have been bullied, so the cycle isn't filled with love, it's filled with hurt people hurting more people. Whew! Some of you may not like what I'm saying right now, but the truth is some of you aren't liking how you're treating yourselves right now either, and that has to stop!

Harvard describes a term, "serve and return," which talks about the interactions in the first years of a child's life that shape their brain architecture. When an infant or young child babbles, gestures, or cries, and an adult responds appropriately with eye contact, words, or a hug, neural connections are built and strengthened in the child's brain that support the development of communication and social skills. Much like a lively game of tennis, volleyball, or Ping-Pong, this back-and-forth is both fun and capacity-building. When caregivers are sensitive and responsive to a young child's signals and needs, they provide an environment rich in serve and return experiences. Because responsive relationships are both expected and essential, their absence is a serious threat to a child's development and well-being. Healthy brain architecture depends on a sturdy foundation built by appropriate input from a child's senses and stable, responsive relationships with caring adults. If an adult's responses to a child are unreliable, inappropriate, or simply absent, the developing architecture of the brain may be disrupted, and subsequent physical, mental, and emotional health may be impaired.

This makes so much sense when we think about the way we are, our children are, our parents are, and so on and so forth. No, I am not playing the blame game that all parents are purposely harming their children. This is just another example that when a child is not in a healthy environment it has long lasting effects that may stay with them through adulthood. An unhealthy environment could look like a mother or father who loves their child so much, but they are struggling mentally, emotionally, spiritually, or all of the above, so they are not capable of providing a well-rounded healthy environment for their child(ren). The environment starts from within, so if you are not feeling good about yourself, how can you help a young innocent child fully feel good about themselves? The work we do on ourselves is crucial, and not just for us but for those we love.

Take a moment to think about that. Keep thinking. Now what about all of what you just read in this chapter is ringing true for you? Jot down the first thought(s) that pops into your head, and it doesn't matter if it seems silly, harsh, or makes your heart beat faster. Don't skip this part. When we put our thoughts on paper, some sort of magical door inside of our heart and head opens up and we can sometimes see things in a new way.

———————————————————————————

———————————————————————————

———————————————————————————

———————————————————————————

———————————————————————————

———————————————————————————

———————————————————————————

———————————————————————————

This is an ongoing challenge for so many people; however, it does not have to be something that cripples you, even though it probably has cost you a lot in your life already. Since we are on the subject of how having low self-image can cost you things, when I asked Jaimie what the challenges she had with her self-image cost her, this was her response:

> One of the biggest things it cost me was healthy relationships. I had friends who would talk about me behind my back, but would hang out with me like they cared about me. After experiencing so much betrayal from friends and ex-boyfriends, it was a while before I felt I could trust people, but while working on my healing I was able to open up to new relationships that I feel good about and that I trust.

I can have conversations with others without worrying about what they think about me, but before it wasn't like that.

I wasted so much energy on caring what others think. I could have been using that energy to enjoy my life, and putting myself out there more to meet people who would accept me for me. At any social event I would go to, I always felt so uncomfortable because of the way I looked. I lost out on enjoying experiences, because I was so worried about what I looked like and what people thought of me. It cost me happiness and creating good memories. I am thankful that is no longer the way I live.

If this sounds anything like you, you are not alone, and it is not too late to heal. If this sounds like how you used to be, congratulations on taking the steps to heal. Now, I would love for you to imagine I am sitting next to you at this very moment, and we are talking about the way you truly see yourself. I want you to think of me as the person you can share all of your thoughts with; the loving, the unloving, the kind, and the ultimate nasty thoughts you have about yourself. Think of me as your safe space, and I've already told you I will never judge you or make you feel less than.

I want to encourage you to set a timer for four minutes and forty-five seconds, because five minutes seem too long. HAHAHA! Next, you will use the space below to write out your thoughts about how you currently view your self-image and how you want to view it moving forward, and one day, a while from now, you will come back to this book, read what you wrote here, and celebrate the self-image growth you have had for yourself between today's date and the date you read it in the future. You totally got this! Don't worry, no one is reading your words except for you, so this is the time to be 100 percent honest with yourself. Honesty leads to healing.

Today's Date & Time: _____

_____

_____

_____

_____

_____

_____

_____

_____

_____

_____

_____

_____

_____

_____

_____

Statements that a woman may say when she views her self-image in a positive or loving way:

* My self-worth is not determined by the size of clothes I wear or the number on the scale.

* I know that I will have love in my life, regardless of what my upbringing was like.

* My friends and family love me for who I am, not if I have money, degrees, or a fancy job.

* These pants don't fit anymore, so it's time to buy new ones that will actually fit. My body deserves clothes that fit well.

* I appreciate the way my body gets me around when I need to move about.

* Just because my first year in business didn't go as planned, doesn't mean that I am a failure. I'll use that year as a learning experience.

* I want my partner to be attracted to who I am, and not base their attraction solely on my looks.

* Working on my health is about becoming better mentally, emotionally, spiritually, and physically. All parts of my health deserve my focus and grace.

* I am just as worthy as anyone else applying for my dream job, so I am going for it!

* Yes, I am a recovering addict, but that doesn't mean that my life is worth less than anyone else's.

* I am not ashamed to say that I want to be a millionaire, and no that doesn't make me a greedy person.

When a woman is confident in her self-image, she:

* Makes decisions that are not based on her looks, but that are based on her desires.

* Doesn't miss out on the opportunity to have fun, take pictures, and celebrate special occasions with family and friends, regardless of how she looks.

* Is confident in who she is as a person, and doesn't allow her employment status, bank account balance, or education level bring her confidence down.

* Puts herself out there for love, friendships, and making new connections for business and pleasure.

* Does not allow others to make her feel less-than because of their own insecurities.

* Spends money on her physical appearance because she wants to, not because she feels she has to.

* Invests in her personal development, her business, and anything else that will benefit her mental health.

JAIMIE'S TRANSFORMATION

We sometimes think if we lose or gain the weight we want, that magically we will feel better about ourselves. That is far from the truth if your mindset isn't right. After taking some time to think about where I was headed in my life, I knew I had some real-life decisions to make. I could not continue on with the way things were, and I had to figure out what was next for me if I wanted to live a better way. Not just with my health, but with my life overall.

There was a point when I got into fitness, joined a gym, and started to love working out. I started getting into the women's fitness classes, and in 2015, I started shadowing those classes to be an instructor. I realized that I had a calling in my life to help people, and this feeling was so strong in me that I could not deny it. That's initially why I wanted to get into nursing: because I wanted to help others.

I started having conversations with other women who were also struggling with their self confidence that was wrapped up in their weight. I understood them and could relate to them. Even though I wasn't making a lot of money in the beginning of my fitness instructor journey, I still loved being able to teach the classes for women. During this time, I decided to add on a second job, because I needed to make some extra money. I knew I could help women in other ways to learn how to love themselves, and this new company I started working for was great with that, especially when it came to women's sexual health. I started to gain confidence the more I worked at the gym, and I was eventually promoted to management at the gym.

It was helping other people love and accept themselves that truly showed me I was on the right path. I still have parts of me that care what others think, and that is my biggest struggle. Imposter syndrome is something that has been a challenge for me for a long time, and it is something I recognize and strive to decrease the levels in which it shows up in my life.

January 2021, I decided to take all of my knowledge of fitness, nutrition, and women's sexual health, and start an online women's fitness business. I knew I could reach a lot of women online, and I was determined to help as many women as I possibly could step into their power. I knew it would also help me step into my own power by helping others do it. When I started my online business, I truly suffered with imposter syndrome, and I knew I needed support to help me with my inner challenges.

March 2021, I hired Denise Marsh as my transformational mindset coach, and she has helped me in more ways than I can count. She taught me how to set boundaries in my life, and why it was a necessity for my overall health. She also helped me to see myself in new ways, so I no longer struggled with needing approval from others. Denise was in my corner then and she still is. I truly believe that her support has helped me with my growth in ways I never even imagined. I feel I have found my inner goddess. WOW! Several years ago, I never would have said that! I don't allow others to walk all over me, because I am a boundary setting QUEEN!! I still have moments where hearing what others think has an effect on me; however, I now have the tools to not let it take over my thoughts. I also understand you can't please everyone. The more successful you become in your life the more haters you're going to have. YES, I said that! I am at a point in my life where I know exactly what I want to do. I know this empire I'm creating is helping women know they are not alone. They can be that powerful person that they truly are that is just waiting to be unleashed.

We are born with an inner goddess, and society and culture can sometimes dim it down. The person that wants higher self-worth is inside of you. You just have to get in there and change your habits. I am proud to say my business is growing, and I know what I want to do with my life. I'm generating money, and I no longer worry about having enough money. All of the relationships that are important to me are thriving. I have solid and supportive women in my life. I also recognize when people are not meant to be in my life, and I know how to deal with that. Remember, I told you I am a boundary setting queen! When I hear other people's stories, I used to think my story didn't matter because it wasn't as deep or as tragic as others, but every story matters. Regardless of what kind of family you were born into, you have a story, and you matter!

Jaimie is so right when she says you have to just get in there and change your habits. It may sound easier saying it than actually doing it, and I understand. It starts with one small and effective step at a time, and by choosing to believe you are capable of making the change. For Jaimie, it was getting to a point of recognizing that she had to take responsibility for the actions in her own life, learning how to trust her inner wisdom and being patient with what that meant for her, getting in the gym to get physically stronger to match her mindset which was also getting stronger, and hiring me as her transformational mindset coach to give her guidance and support on her mindset and self-love journey. Did you read what she did? Even though her biggest challenge initially seemed to be about her weight, it was more so about her mindset. She had to work on healing herself mentally, emotionally, spiritually, and physically to get the results she desired to live more purposefully and with love and grace for herself—not just physically, everyone! Read that last sentence again please! So many people put so much work into their physical appearance when they are struggling with their self-image, and that is not the solution. Doing the work on your overall health is where the deep and effective results will make the difference.

The biggest changes Jaimie has noticed internally is that she is less stressed, her anxiety decreased, and she is able to sleep peacefully at night, which was rare for her in the past, because she was worried about money or whatever was going on in her life that she didn't feel good about. Jaimie is now able to trust her inner wisdom, show herself love instead of shame, and wear whatever she wants without caring what other people will think about her.

Her confidence has increased, she feels good in her body, and she amped up her love for wearing heels and being the tallest person in the room. Before she felt she was towering over people, or worried that people would judge her for wearing heels just because she was tall. Now, she is confident walking into any room, and enjoys being tall. She embraces what makes her different, where in the past she would try to hide from it.

When it comes to the changes Jaimie has experienced externally since being on her self-love journey, she has relationships that are real because she sets boundaries, and she is OK with relationships ending that no longer serve her. She used to get down when people would unfollow or block her on social media, but now that doesn't bother her when that happens. She has discovered healthier ways to communicate with those closest to her, and have conversations about topics that in the past would make her uncomfortable. In the past she felt she had to change herself to be accepted by others, and now she owns who she is and the person she chooses to be with will have to accept who she is. She knows exactly the path she wants to take, and she's doing it without feeling the need for anyone's approval about it.

Jaimie is a person just like you who wants to be accepted, loved, and seen. The big, huge realization for Jaimie was that she had to first learn how to accept, love, and see herself as the woman she wanted to be. You have the same powers and capability as Jaimie has. Are you willing to do the work to have a stronger outlook on your self-image? The tools are available for you to make that happen!

A LOVING R.A.W. MESSAGE FROM JAIMIE TO YOU:

Everything is going to be OK. This is a moment in time, and everything you are going to experience and have experienced is a lesson and will make you stronger. Stop trying to please everyone else, and listen to your inner voice. The loving voice inside that's speaking to you is the real you. Your intuition will guide you, so you don't need to listen to what others are saying that doesn't align with what you want. Trusting your intuition will guide you down the path of your choosing.

SELFIE TIME!

When we are increasing the love meter on our self-image, we have to work on our spiritual, mental, emotional, and physical health. This will mean something different to each individual. What do they mean to you, and what is one step you can take today to increase your love meter with your self-image in these areas? For example, one thing I do for my spiritual health is meditate daily, and for my emotional health, I create and commit to boundaries. Now, it's your turn!

Spiritual Health

_____

_____

_____

_____

_____

_____

_____

_____

_____

_____

Mental Health

_____

_____

_____

_____

_____

_____

_____

_____

_____

_____

Emotional Health

_____

_____

_____

_____

_____

_____

_____

_____

_____

Physical Health

_____

_____

_____

_____

_____

_____

_____

_____

_____

BRITTANY VICK'S SELF-IMAGE STORY

FROM DIMMING HER LIGHT TO SHINING BRIGHT

**Here is a story about a woman who went from being afraid
of shining too bright to owning her truest self!**

For so long I felt I wasn't worthy of living a good life or a life
I deserved. Certain situations would happen in my life that
would cause me to believe that I wasn't meant to be happy. There was a time when so many challenges were hitting
me at once. My husband became really sick, my brother
passed away, and life was becoming extremely overwhelming for me. I truly felt I shouldn't be happy because bad
things were happening in my life and to the people I loved.
I've suffered from anxiety and low self-confidence for so
long, and it took a while to realize that this was all related
to how I saw myself. My self-image has been a real struggle
for years, and the term self-image wasn't something that I
heard other people talking about. If anything, I thought it
had to do with how we see ourselves physically, which was
also something I would be hard on myself about. Self-image isn't just how we see ourselves physically, it's how we
see ourselves overall. As far back as I can remember, I was
afraid of shining too bright around certain people, because I felt I would be judged. Anytime I would accomplish
something, I thought if I talked about it, people wouldn't

like me, or they would have negative thoughts about me. So, I dimmed myself to not have others dislike me. Truth was, I didn't like who I was sometimes, so I thought others felt the same.

I've always known that I am an introvert, but I felt that I had to be an extrovert in order for people to like me and want to be around me. When I was around my family, I felt confident about being myself. I didn't have to be this extra bubbly person that I truly wasn't. When it came to business events, or social settings around people I didn't know too well, that's when I felt I had to be extra high-energy and bubbly and that wasn't true to me. I felt like I had to put on a show and shine bright in order to be accepted. I do have a bubbly nature, but not in all situations or with all types of people.

During the years I was challenged with low self-confidence and poor self-image, I imagined someone with high self-confidence being the life of the party, high-energy, and someone everyone was drawn to. Well, I was not like that, but believed I had to be like that in order to have friends. I am more reserved and introverted, and for so long I thought something was wrong with that. No one ever told me that I wasn't a confident person or that being introverted was bad, these were just thoughts that I created in my head. I would have constant thoughts about me being an introvert and not being confident about that part of me. Don't get me wrong, there were many areas in my life that I did feel confident in, but the areas where I didn't affected me in major ways.

Going through years of low self-confidence, low self-esteem, and poor self-image cost me:

* Feeling unworthy because I felt like I wasn't good enough for people. I always thought, "Would people like me?" or "Will they want to be my friend if I acted how I truly am?" It brought me down when I was trying to be that other person.

* My energy, because I would be so exhausted from trying to be someone I wasn't that it would bring my spirits down.

* Having high anxiety for years to the point where I would want to withdraw from people and events because I knew putting on the facade would drain me. It would take me days to refill my energy from those times. I like to have my time to decompress, and I used to have guilt about wanting to spend time alone when I would travel or go to big events. I would think that people wouldn't think I was fun because I wasn't hanging out with them and I wanted to do things by myself. I felt that people wouldn't want to invite me to places, because they would think that I wasn't fun.

One year I decided to attend one of Denise's R.A.W. retreats, and this retreat focused on healing past wounds and trauma in order to live more presently and purposefully. I had heard about her transformational retreats, so I had an idea of what to expect, but I didn't expect to dig as deep as we did. Going into the retreat, I knew I wanted to focus on increasing my confidence in the areas it was lacking in, and learn healthier ways of truly seeing and accepting myself for who I am. During the retreat with Denise, she helped me to dig deep to pull things out of me that I didn't even know were there by asking me questions no one has asked me. She also pushed me in a way no one has ever pushed me before. Was it challenging? Yes! Was it worth it? Yes!

One of the realizations I experienced was that the thoughts I was having were beliefs I no longer wanted, and I was in control of changing those thoughts. It was a matter of believing that I was worthy of a good life, that I was more than enough as who I am and not who I was trying to be, that I am proud of my accomplishments, and that I don't have to dim my light for anyone. By continuing to work with Denise and putting the work into myself, I was feeling more confident with being my true self and being more loving towards myself. I now believe I am a great person, a great wife, and one day I will be a great mom. When I started being true to who I am and stopped trying to be a super bubbly, outgoing, extroverted person, I started feeling confident in living authentically as my introverted self. I know people will love me for me, and not who I think I'm supposed to be. I feel calmer and more confident around my friends, and I realized my friends do love my introverted personality. People are drawn to the type of person I am, and owning that increased my confidence. I noticed when I was trying to take on a different type of personality, I was anxious, and not confident in certain settings. Trying to be this big bright light all of the time was draining me. Now that I have adapted to being the calm person that I am, I can be more confident in all scenarios. I don't feel like I'm being fake or putting on a show. I am ME and I love all of me!

What has changed for me since truly owning who I am, accepting who I am, and loving myself in new ways:

* I am more confident, and I feel that I am truly worthy of the life I want to live. I can shine bright when I want to, and I can be who I am and not feel there are drawbacks to being my true self. I can do my own thing, and not worry if others like me.

* A few friendships ended when I started living authentically, but I also gained the right friends at the same time.

* I'm more confident in my relationship with my husband, and confident in knowing the direction that we are headed.

* My relationships with my friends feel better on my end, because I can truly be myself and not be in my head if they want to be around me or not. I'm more relaxed when I'm with my friends because I'm not constantly thinking about whether they enjoy being around me.

* My business has always been successful, but I feel more confident in my business. I am even attracting the right type of people in my business, and I feel that my changes are inspiring others.

* People are noticing my transformation, and that is because I changed from within.

* I work less and make more money, and my team has grown in many ways.

* The internal thoughts I tell myself daily are definitely making a difference in myself and in the people I am surrounding myself with. After attending Denise's retreat, I learned how to challenge my negative self-talk. I still have those thoughts pop up, but now I know how to challenge those thoughts and turn them around to be positive. In the past I would truly believe my negative thoughts and wouldn't know how to stop them.

Now I am thankful to have the tools to change that.

* I used to be scared to post my accomplishments on social media, because I would feel judged, or worried that people would think I was conceited. Now I know that when I post about my accomplishments and my happiness, it is inspiring to others and I am proud of what I have done. I don't need to be ashamed of that or hide it because others may feel a certain way about it. I was afraid to shine my own light in the past in my own way, and now I feel so free being able to share my joy with others. I now feel I can live my life and people can like me for me, or not!

A LOVING R.A.W. MESSAGE FROM BRITTANY TO YOU:

Deep down inside you truly do have the key to unlock your full potential, even if you may not realize it right now. Dig deep and know that you are worthy; you're deserving of living a life you love and desire. Unleash the YOU that you feel is trapped inside that wants to get out. Start living the life that is authentic. Your past doesn't define your future. When you truly believe in your worth and confidence in yourself, that is going to give you the motivation you need to keep pushing forward even on the days you don't feel like it. When you are more confident, you start to feel more worthy! You can break through the barrier that you have been feeling stuck in. It starts with believing in yourself and being true to you!

CHAPTER FIVE

SELF-SATISFACTION

CAN I PUT MYSELF FIRST?

DEFINITION

The Britannica Dictionary describes self-satisfaction as, "A feeling of being very pleased or satisfied with yourself and what you have done."

Another definition I want to connect to this chapter is about life-satisfaction. According to the highly regarded life-satisfaction scholar, Ruut Veenhoven, in an article in Positive Psychology, "Life satisfaction is the degree to which a person positively evaluates the overall quality of his/her life as a whole. In other words, how much the person likes the life he/she leads."

In another article titled "Self-Satisfaction: A Key To Success" the subject was explained this way: "To lead a happy and healthy life Self Satisfaction plays a key and vital role. Self-satisfaction should be achieved in all aspects of life. Achieving self-satisfaction lies within oneself. Balancing physical and emotional issues can lead us to achieve self-satisfaction."

In the words of your friend, me, self-satisfaction is a gosh darn non-negotiable to living your life!

know you were hoping for a story, so of course I will give it to you! Meet my friend, Stacey Bauch, who decided she was done feeling unsatisfied in her life.

We go through life thinking there's a way we should live, should do, all of these "shoulds." My spiritual therapist used to tell me not to "should" on myself, and I really loved that. We feel that we have to live up to someone's "should," and that's why a lot of people don't do certain things in life. I want to highlight that there is that inner voice that wants to guide us somewhere else, and our gut is telling us to just do it. Yes, it may be scary, but you just do it.

I was doing so well in every aspect in my life. I was in a relationship, was doing well in my career, getting the accolades, had tons of friends, made great money, and yet I felt like crap. I kept thinking, "Why am I depressed.?" I stopped taking birth control, which I felt affected my moods. Then I started having shame because I was depressed, but felt I should feel blessed for all of the great things going on in my life. I didn't want to take any medications, which is why I got off of birth control. I wanted to find out what was wrong with me. My doctor recommended going to a counselor, and during this time I was dating someone. I started going weekly to a counselor, and the questions she asked me started to unravel things in my life and from my past. There was depression, anxiety, and alcoholism in my family, and unraveling certain things actually made me feel better. There was a reason I was feeling the way I was, and things started making sense. I started realizing the relationship I was in was toxic. I used to think everything was my fault, and that was very tiring. My partner made me feel like everything was my fault, and so I kept trying to "fix" myself. I was allowing people to mistreat me, but I didn't realize it for a while.

My ex was supercritical about everything I did, and I didn't see this as a huge issue until I started counseling. One day I was changing the litter for my bunnies, and my ex walked by, and I remember being so nervous of him watching me, because I knew he had a certain way of cleaning the litter. I ended up spilling some of the litter, and he made a judgmental comment about it and told me what I did wrong. I thought to myself that this is not OK, and I don't even feel comfortable in my own home. It felt awful being criticized. I knew I wouldn't want anyone else to feel that way, so why should I feel that way?

I wanted to change my outlook on myself and my life, so I started implementing different things to help me. I started reading Gabby Bernstein, who I love. Going through Gabby's book helped me to see things in new ways, and I started to make changes in my own life. I realized while living my best life that I was not the problem. I still wasn't feeling good about the relationship with my boyfriend, my mom, and even some of my friends. I wasn't putting myself first, and at this time I was a people-pleaser. So, after attending counseling for a year, I found a spiritual healer. I got to a point where I needed someone else to help me on my self-love journey. I wanted to go deeper, and through an introduction I met my spiritual healer. I was having a hard time grasping what I needed to do to feel better, because again my life looked great on the outside, but something still wasn't right on the inside. There was a time when I wouldn't want to get out of bed. I had quit my teaching job and went full time with my new business. I was naturally a happy person, but I couldn't bring my bright sunshine all of the time and I felt it was expected. There were times when I would do things in my business and people would comment that I'm an overachiever, or that what I did was so incredible, and I just couldn't see it. I never felt good enough for myself. I always felt I could do more and be more.

Stacey, I feel you and I know so many other people can relate to you as well. It seems to be the norm for a lot of people to make it appear that everything in their life looks good on the outside, when on the inside they're unhappy, depressed, anxious, unfulfilled, or feeling like they're dying. It's like putting a beautiful new outfit on the guy from that '90s show, *Tales from the Crypt*. You're basically covering up something you feel is hideous and scary. Wanting to feel satisfied and fulfilled in our lives is not a bad thing. It is actually a beautiful and honorable way to show appreciation for the life you get to live each and every day. Why the heck would you not want to be satisfied with this one known life you are living?! That's what's happening to many people. It happened to me, Stacey, and others who are reading this book right now.

When a woman is not experiencing self-satisfaction in her life, she may say statements like this:

* I can't remember the last time I did something just for myself.

* I'll be happy when I make more money.

* Everyone else's needs always come before mine.

* Why can't I be happy? I'm never happy.

* My life seems almost perfect to everyone else, so why do I feel miserable?

* If I lose/gain weight, I'll finally be happy with myself.

* My life is a hot mess express.

* If it weren't for _____ , I could have more fun in my life.

* My (parents, partner, children) are a huge disappointment to me.

* Maybe if I move to another state, I will stop being so depressed.

When you were reading the statements above, did any of them sound like you, or how you used to feel? Was it one statement, a few, or all of them that you related to? We've come so far in this book journey, so we are not about to beat ourselves up over some statements that may or may not play on repeat in our minds. This is about recognizing where you are on your self-love journey, what needs to change, and making the commitment to do what it takes to live out the rest of your life with love, joy, peace, fun. and pure satisfaction!

If your happiness is tied to an outcome, you won't ever find long-term satisfaction, because you'll always chase the next milestone, the next pay increase, the next fitness goal, the next award, the next relationship, the next social media hype. The moment you hit the finish line, you'll experience a temporary high, and then set out for the next thing that will supposedly make you happy. Even though chasing goals can be a fun part of your life, self-satisfaction isn't meant to be a goal; self-satisfaction is meant to be a sustainable and stable part of your life.

Allow me to break it down for you a little bit more. Self-satisfaction comes from within, and not the Louis Vuitton store or the brand-new Tesla. Am I knocking Louis Vuitton and Tesla? Ummm, nope! I'm simply saying that sometimes people will seek out achieving satisfaction by buying things, earning things, winning things, or even giving things to others. "Things" don't bring pure self-satisfaction; however, they may bring you some fun, temporary happiness, comfort, or excitement. If you really want to be satisfied, make more time and space in your life for the small pleasures. A small pleasure could include taking a leisurely walk on a beautiful day and honoring the fact that you have a way to get around your neighborhood. Another example of a small pleasure is calling a friend just because, and having some good belly laughs with them. FYI, good belly laughs are priceless, and so good for the soul!

It also helps when we choose gratitude over complaining, and to stop the cycle of complaining, either change your surroundings, your mindset, or both. I get it, this may be one of those moments where you're thinking to yourself that this is easier said than done, but is it? That same energy you put into complaining is the same energy you can put into showing some gratitude. Here is an example of what gratitude is not: "Thank you for cooking dinner for us tonight; however, it would have been nice if you would have cooked the steaks like I asked you to." Here is an example of what gratitude is: "Thank you for cooking dinner for us tonight. I've had a full day, and you cooking dinner is helping me in so many ways." This is a simple example, but you get the point! When we have more gratitude in what we do, what we have, who we are, and where we are, we add more satisfaction to our lives.

Think of it this way, complaining decreases your appreciation and satisfaction in the areas you're complaining about, and gratitude increases your appreciation and satisfaction in the areas you're showing gratitude in. I am fully aware that there are times when it may seem that having gratitude is tough, especially after a major loss of a loved one, an illness, money challenges, and this list can go on and on. I am also fully aware that sometimes life can feel sucky; however, when you stay in a state of complaining or the victim mentality, it does not help your overall quality of life in any way. There is so much to be grateful for, and there are also so many ways to change the way you see yourself in your life to increase your satisfaction levels.

Over the years I have had more jobs than I have fingers and toes, and some of them I truly enjoyed. There was this one job I had that was pretty decent, but what I liked most about it were the people I worked with and that was about it. Every morning I would drive almost two hours to my job, and every morning I had to pump myself up to get in a good mindset to not call off. Even though I enjoyed my co-workers, it wasn't my dream job and I was not that happy with my income. Yes, it paid my bills plus I had benefits, so I was grateful about that, but there wasn't much money left over after all of my bills and expenses were paid for the month. I just kept telling myself I would be happier with this job once I started making more money. This company would do performance reviews every twelve to twenty-four months, and I wanted to make sure I was doing everything possible to get a great raise. The day of my review I remember thinking how I would finally make enough to start saving more money, and eventually be able to purchase a more reliable car, and finally be happier about working there. Long story short, they were giving me a twenty-five cent raise. You can re-read that last part if you must, but it is not a typo. I worked there for over a year, didn't call off (even though I wanted to almost daily), did my job well, and never got into trouble. I was so confused, disappointed, and, by the end of the day, I was angry.

The truth is it wasn't just my job that I wasn't satisfied in: I wasn't satisfied in the relationship with my boyfriend at that time; my social life was almost non-existent because I never had money to do anything fun; I was lacking energy because I was on the latest fad diet; and I was just not a happy person. People still seemed to like being around me, but I couldn't stand being around myself most days. Change for me didn't come for many years, because I didn't understand that for me to feel satisfied, happy, and peaceful, I had to get that from myself and not expect everyone and everything else to give it to me. Don't rely on "things" or people to make your life complete

This makes me think of the saying, "Keeping up with the Joneses." It is literally plastered all over the internet, social media, magazines, email ads, and conversations with others that in order to be happy or complete, you need certain parts of your life to look a certain way.

Any of this sound familiar?

* My company has this new incentive, and I know that if I am one of the people to earn it, I will finally feel that all of the hard work and extra hours I've been putting in was worth it.

* Ugh, my life is a mess! I feel like absolute crap, so maybe I'll go blow some money at the mall and then devour that pint of ice-cream that's been calling my name. If that doesn't work, I'll just drink myself to sleep. There is no way I'm calling my friends about this, because they think my life is going great, and I want to keep it that way.

* You have to have a jaw-dropping wedding, invite all of the people you like and don't like, have the most expensive gown (or at least a gown that looks expensive), the best-catered food, the most awesome DJ, and the breathtaking venue just so for one day you can have people say how amazing it was.

Now, please don't try to look up my address to send me hate mail, because you think I'm judging you or bashing the beautiful wedding you had or have planned. I am talking about those who feel they NEED this in order to feel happy or a sense of fulfillment. I absolutely love going to weddings, and if a big shindig is what you want, then please invite me! I'm also asking you to be mindful of taking notice of why you're doing what you're doing. Is it because this is what you've truly always dreamed of, or are you doing this because you think you "should," or are you trying to impress someone?

Too often we try to satisfy everyone else around us: our children, parents/those who raised us, bosses, friends, society, clients, and the list goes on and on. To truly feel satisfied, start by being yourself—your real self, and not the self you think you should be—and then take some time to figure out what decisions you want to make for yourself and how you want to live your own life on your terms, and not the ones made up by everyone else.

Does this sound easy to you?
(Circle one below.)

YES, IT DOES!

UMMM, NO, SO I'M NOT GOING TO EVEN TRY.

MAYBE, BUT WHAT IF I MESS UP?

If you circled, "YES, IT DOES," Great! What's the first step you're taking to increase your self-satisfaction?

_____

_____

_____

_____

_____

_____

If you circled, "UMMM, NO, SO I'M NOT GOING TO EVEN TRY," close this book and throw it away. Just kidding! But seriously, why is this your answer?

_____

_____

_____

_____

_____

_____

If you circled, "MAYBE, BUT WHAT IF I MESS UP," congratulations on wanting to try. Now, let me reassure you that there is no way you can mess up, as long as you take some sort of action. What is one loving action step you can take within the next twenty-four hours that will increase your self-satisfaction?

_____

_____

_____

_____

_____

_____

_____

This journey of life that we are each experiencing in our own way deserves attention, appreciation, and loving growth work. When we don't put attention, appreciation, and loving growth work into ourselves, we suffer in many ways, and that is so unnecessary. When I asked Stacey in what ways she suffered while going through her challenges, this is what she said:

* My mental health suffered... I would have brain fog and fatigue often. I wasn't living in my truth, and my body was starting to deteriorate. I wasn't unhealthy, but I felt unhealthy and bad all of the time. I was in my late twenties and early thirties, and felt older than my age.

* I was talking down to myself a lot.

* I was never good enough for me. No one told me this, but I told myself.

* I was depressed and anxious more times than I can count.

Are some of you thinking that these words are not from Stacey, but from yourself? Were you nodding your head as you were reading the statements above, because you can totally relate? We all know talking down to yourself is a big, Big, BIG challenge for many people. This is learned behavior. You were not born to think poorly of yourself. Your environment taught you who to be, how to be, and what to be. As a fully functional adult you get to decide NOW who you want to be, how you want to be, and what you want to be. The blame game is not something that people who are self-satisfied do. When you have pure satisfaction in your life, you also own your actions—all of them! You can no longer blame your upbringing, your teachers, your ex, your children, the government, religion, or the many times you swiped your credit card. You are human, and you are allowed to have a past that you aren't proud of, and you also are allowed to create a present and future that you are proud of. So, what's stopping you from being fully satisfied with your life? Notice, I did not say who. HAHAHAHA! Oh, and let me give you the answer to the question. Nothing is stopping you, but excuses, self-pity, and a few past shameful moments. Time out for that! What to do is already within you, and asking for support may be part of your solution.

Let's see what happened with Stacey!

My healing journey started in 2016 when I realized I needed answers. I was not OK with the way I was feeling, and I was determined to do something about it. In 2017, I started counseling. In 2018, I hired a spiritual healer. Soon after, I hired a business coach as well as a mindset coach. I attended several retreats I felt would benefit my spiritual, mental, and emotional health. These were group retreats, and I even attended a one-on-one retreat. One of the group retreats and the one-on-one retreat I attended were with Denise, who I also worked with on mindset for a few months. Having multiple ways of support was important to me, and I knew that investing in myself was what would help me to grow. Along with the support and new tools I had from coaches and retreats, I also listened to helpful Audible books whenever I could, and even with my busy schedule I knew I couldn't make any excuses. I started listening to podcasts that made me feel good and raised my spirits. Since I was healing within myself, the relationships I was in were also healing. I made choices that benefited my true desires for myself and my health, which included moving away by myself to a new state, ending relationships that I needed to end, being open to new relationships that felt good, and taking more time to enjoy the simple pleasures in my life. I was used to always being go, go, go, and I found peace and joy in slowing down in certain areas in my life. One of my favorite authors and speakers is Gabby Bernstein, and she said that everything is an assignment in our lives, and we have to learn from our experiences. Right now, I'm a mom, and so I'm learning a new way of navigating my life and also making time to reflect on the reasons I did certain things in my past. I can say with certainty that I am on a path of self-love and living my life in pure satisfaction.

Besides me, who else is smiling after reading Stacey's transformation? Stacey, you did the dang thing! There is usually a tipping point that we get to where we either say enough is enough, or we accept the displeasure that we feel about our lives. Stacey chose the enough is enough route, and because of her choices other people benefited from it too. That wasn't her goal, but it happened anyway. Her relationships became stronger and healthier. That's the beauty of our connections to one another. Our happiness is contagious, and there have been studies about this. A new study by researchers at Harvard University and the University of California, San Diego, documents how happiness spreads through social networks. They found that when a person becomes happy, a friend living close by has a 25 percent higher chance of becoming happy themselves. A spouse experiences an 8 percent increased chance and for next-door neighbors, it's 34 percent. "Everyday interactions we have with other people are definitely contagious, in terms of happiness," says Nicholas Christakis, a professor at Harvard Medical School and an author of the study. Perhaps more surprising, Christakis says, is that the effect extends beyond the people we come into contact with. When one person becomes happy, the social network effect can spread up to three degrees—reaching friends of friends. This also goes the other way, that our misery can be contagious as well. Misery may love company, but happiness and joy want you to move in! Yes, I just laughed at myself. HEHEHE! That's the other thing, those who have strong self-satisfaction know where to put their time and energy, and they don't sweat the small stuff.

When a woman experiences self-satisfaction in her life she:

* Knows that investing in her well-being is an act of real self-care.

* Takes time to rest and slow down, and her mind and body appreciate her for it and don't get overwhelmed.

* Does not spend time putting others down, but instead will find ways to lift others up.

* Loves treating herself to vacations and gifts because she enjoys them and not because she feels she needs them to fill a void.

* Spends her time focused on her own actions, and not wasting her time and energy being frustrated by the way other people are acting.

* Understands the blame game is a losing battle, and instead learns from past mistakes and challenges.

When I asked Stacey what changes she has noticed internally since living a more self-satisfied life, she responded:

* When I make a decision, even if it's uncomfortable, I don't back away from it.

* In the past when something came up that I didn't want to address, I would not want to follow through. I don't hide from uncomfortable situations. This still is uncomfortable at times for me, but now I recognize it and I can still follow through with it.

* I didn't have the confidence in myself to make the right decisions in the past, and now I trust myself to make the right decisions.

* I learned from my past and can speak positively about the challenges I had, instead of dwelling on them in a negative way.

Stacey also shared the changes she noticed externally since making some loving changes in her life:

* I'm living in a different area with sunshine.

* I take chances on myself, and experience life differently.

* I'm not trying to compete with others and be the best.

* Being a new mom has caused me to slow down, and I'm no longer wondering what's next.

* Sometimes the thought pops up in my head that I am not doing enough, and now I can reassure myself that I am doing enough.

* I am choosing my actions based on what feels good for me, and not what others want me to do.

* My life feels more purposeful, and not for someone else but for what I need.

* My ego is still there and says I need to be number one and make more money and go a mile a minute, but that's not what I need anymore, and I can recognize when my ego shows up and make a decision that is not ego-based.

Stacey, I know you are so proud of yourself, and truly living your best life now! You created a new environment filled with love, grace, and sunshine for your son by creating that environment for yourself. When we do what's good for us, others will benefit from that as well. When we take care of ourselves, nurture our life experiences, and trust in our intuition to make the right decisions, our lives truly are more fulfilled, purposeful, and joyful!

This is true for each person reading this book. Having self-satisfaction is not just for the lucky ones, or the ones who went to college, or even the ones who were born on a day when there was a full moon. This is something that is available to every living human, which includes you. I have good news for you! Just by reading this book and participating in the activities, you are committing to growing in whatever way you want and need most. Remember, there is no magic spell, secret pill, or sacred ritual that will make your life picture-perfect. However, there are ways you can make changes to increase more of what you want and decrease what you no longer want. Many of them are placed throughout this book! You just have to believe that change is possible for you, that you are worthy of living in a better way, and that you are a lovable and loving person who deserves to live life on purpose and with true satisfaction!

A LOVING R.A.W. MESSAGE FROM STACEY TO YOU:

Get quiet, put down your phone, turn off the TV, and ask yourself what you are thinking about. Know that your feelings are valid; however, don't identify yourself with a feeling. For example, when you may say, "I am depressed," you are not depressed, you are feeling depressed. You are experiencing a feeling, and know that it will pass.

Do something for yourself, and get outside. Connecting to nature, even if it's outside on your porch, can switch how you're feeling if you're experiencing a feeling you don't like at the moment. Take some time to ask yourself, "If you could do anything, what would it be, even if it's small?" Don't decide what you want to do based on what others will think about it. I used to always wonder what my mother would think about my choices, or my boyfriend, or whoever. So, I wasn't doing what I wanted most of the time, and now I am doing what I want. So, ask yourself what you need and want most in your life right now. Don't scroll on your phone to find out what you need. Get quiet, and ask yourself.

Be open to opportunities!

SELFIE TIME!

For repetition's sake and because I thought it was fun, let's repeat the exercise from earlier... with a couple of tweaks.

Does living a self-satisfied life sound easy to you?
(Circle one below.)

Mindset Tip: whenever you say something is easy, your body relaxes and you're able to find solutions. Whenever you say something is hard, your body tenses and thinks about the problem or the challenge.

YES, IT DOES!

ABSOLUTELY IT DOES!

YES, BUT WHAT IF I MESS UP?

If you circled, "YES, IT DOES," great! What's the first step you're taking to increase your self-satisfaction within the next hour?

_____

_____

_____

_____

If you circled, "ABSOLUTELY IT DOES," what are the first and second steps you are taking within the next twenty-four hours to increase your self-satisfaction?

_____

_____

_____

_____

_____

_____

If you circled, "YES, BUT WHAT IF I MESS UP," we all have doubts every now and then, especially when it comes to something new. Now, let me reassure you again that there is no way you can mess up, as long as you take some sort of action. What is one loving action step you can take each day over the next five days that will increase your self-satisfaction?

_____

_____

_____

_____

_____

_____

KAYLA KOEP'S SELF-SATISFACTION STORY

FROM CARETAKER TO CARING FOR HERSELF!

Here is a story about a woman who went from caring for everyone else to living an OH SO GOOD life just for herself!

I am a very good caretaker. In fact, I've been caring for more years in my life than I haven't... Starting as a young pre-teen I began caring for others as a way to find purpose and peace in my life. After graduation, I launched into college mode and felt called to study ministry (which is essentially serving others). It's now been over twenty years since college, and I've made a career out of serving others. Don't get me wrong: serving and caring for others is a rewarding and honorable way to live in the world. However, what is wrong, or rather, where I went wrong, was putting myself and my satisfaction and own self-love on the back burner (if it was even on the stove at all). I was burnt out, resentful, and unfulfilled.

I met Denise the year of her very first R.A.W. retreat. I was burnt out, depleted of self-love, resentful in my relationships and work, and also really hopeful I may find my way towards a better way to live. I was in a relationship where I set my needs aside to care for my partner and his family. I was working full-time as a household manager/family assistant for a high-profile family (a job I always hoped for), and on the outside things looked pretty dandy for me.

During one of the sharing circles on the retreat, I remember saying: "You know, I really just miss myself. I miss ME more." This declaration, I believe, was the launch pad for my future takeoff into spaces yet unknown. I left the retreat feeling known, loved, supported, and determined to put ME first. Denise was my co-captain in this rocket ship called life, and with her by my side, I began to dream again. I started to journal again. I began taking myself on dates. I began speaking up when I needed to. I began wearing what I LOVED and not what I thought my partner would like more. I also began to consider what life could be like if I was living from the heart, and out of fullness.

In college, I penned a life mission statement. It was: to help others discover how they're wired and help them live accordingly.

Twenty years later, I am discovering who I am. I'm leaning into a calling and desire to be a companion with people as a spiritual director (Yep, you guessed it... I went back to school for what I originally studied). I moved in with my partner and moved out and left my partner. (Growing is painful.) I continued to work in my same field but changed jobs. I started building my own care team which currently consists of a therapist and spiritual director. My whole life is getting a makeover, and it's beginning with Me. Me first...

What my past challenge cost me:

* Self-love.
* Self-acceptance.
* My overall health and well-being.
* Opportunities.
* Joy and happiness.

What has changed for me internally and externally:

I am marching to MY own beat, and not the beat of others. I am strengthening my emotional muscles and boundaries. I am healing my own inner-child. I am forgiving myself and others. I am living a life I am proud of and feel most alive in. These internal workings have impacted my relationships with dating partners, my friendships, and my family. I live in my own cozy city space in Minneapolis, and am committed to learning and growing and dreaming. As I begin to put myself first, I open myself up to being truly present and being a changing force in the world.

A LOVING **R.A.W.** MESSAGE FROM KAYLA TO YOU:

Girl, you matter. What you need matters. What you believe matters. What you have to say and give to the world matters. If you don't yet believe that quite fully for yourself, let me believe it with you. It is a worthy, noble, life-giving act to give yourself the most love and care before anyone else. It's like the flight attendants say: "Please secure your own mask first before assisting others."

CHAPTER SIX

SELF-LOVE

DO YOU KNOW HOW TO LOVE YOUR SELFIE?

You have taken the journey through this book with me and the women who have shared parts of their stories, and we have dug into what the SELFIES actually mean, how they show up in our lives, how they are instilled in us, and how we can improve and increase them. When we come to the realization that our self-worth, self-validation, self-confidence, self-image, and self-satisfaction all lead to something so powerful, which is the love we have for ourselves, we start to see how they impact our lives. This is not something that is always modeled to us in our younger years, or throughout the course of our lives. Most times, it's the complete opposite that is shown to us, which is to be insecure, to put everyone and everything else ahead of yourself, that having boundaries is mean and rude, that the shape and weight of your body defines your attractiveness, and that you have to prove your worth through accolades, awards, and money. None of that is true, and we cannot let old unhealthy beliefs that were instilled in us from people, events, and situations be the crutch we lean on for the rest of our lives. It is time to take ownership of who you are choosing to be, and how you are choosing to live the rest of your life. One of the best ways to do this is with love.

When we think about how we learn to love ourselves and others, we discover that we learn these love lessons from sooooooooooo many ways. We learn from watching the bigger humans, a.k.a. adults, who raise us or who we spend our time with as children. Sometimes the lessons we learn about self-love or love in general from adults aren't really healthy or true definitions of love for others or love for ourselves.

When a woman doesn't know how to love herself, she may:

* Have destructive behavior, and cause harm to herself or others.

* Live in victim mode the majority of her days.

* Talk meanly to herself about her body, instead of feeling gratitude for her functioning limbs, organs and other body parts that help her to live her life.

* Feel she needs to change her appearance in order to be accepted by others.

* Believe she needs others to love her in order to feel validated and worthy.

* Justify why she remains in an abusive relationship (with an intimate partner, a friend, or a family member).

* Feel that her weight or clothing size determines if she's lovable or not.

* Have thoughts of ending her life, or feel that her life is pointless.

* Go through the motions of just "living," but not feeling real joy or happiness.

* Have friends who are not positive influences, and who also struggle with self-love.

* Blame herself when someone mistreats her.

* Feel she is not worthy of being happy or living a good life.

By now you know the drill. So, which of the above statements have been true for you at one point in your life? Which statements are still true for you today? Is there anything else right now you want to get out of your head and onto paper? Here you go!

_____

_____

_____

_____

_____

_____

_____

_____

Another way we may learn how to view love is through songs. As I was doing my research on love songs about others and ourselves, I came across an article talking about the history of love songs. In his 2016 lecture on the subject of his book Love Songs: The Hidden History, Ted Gioia explained how love ballads emerged in the eighth-century tunes of medieval female Arab slaves in Spain. Some four hundred years later, European troubadours spread their songs of longing, an early indication that pleasure and pain are natural bedfellows in a love song (Gioia, 2016).

It has been estimated that more than one hundred million love songs have been recorded, and the variety is staggering. There are songs about new love (a rich vein that everyone from Elvis Presley to Ed Sheeran has mined); songs for time-tested devotion (such as Ella Fitzgerald and Louis Armstrong's duet on the Gershwin classic "Our Love Is Here To Stay"); break-up songs (Taylor Swift's "We Are Never Ever Getting Back Together" sold seven million copies); songs of devotion (Whitney Houston's version of Dolly Parton's "I Will Always Love You" is one of the most popular tracks ever); and songs about making up and forgiveness (Elton John's "Sorry Seems To Be The Hardest Word").

As I kept digging to see how many songs have been recorded about self-love, the information that popped up was only talking about the top ten or thirteen best songs about loving ourselves. There was an article giving a list of the top fifty songs about loving yourself, and seriously they were really reaching with a ton of the songs. Most of them were not really about loving ourselves, but about getting revenge on someone who left you and now being able to have someone else who deserves you. Some were more about loving our physical bodies and finding your own pleasure. Now, don't get me wrong, I'm all about loving on ALL of ourselves; however, why aren't there more songs about why self-love is important (actually MORE important than finding love in someone else)? Isn't that interesting—or is it—that there are over 100 million songs about loving someone else, but not a solid fifty songs can be found about loving our own selves!? Does this not tell you about the message that is and has been going around the world since the dawn of time, that being in love with someone else or finding that undying love in another human is what life is all about. I guess it does seem quite right that many of us are confused about how to view love. It's literally in most of the songs that we listen to that our life is not complete until we find that one true love, or that our life is over if our one true love leaves us. Geesh! This is a big eye opener... or is it?

It makes me think about going through a breakup when I was in high school and playing "*No Ordinary Love*" by Sade on repeat and crying on the phone with my best friend, Emanuel. My mom burst in my room holding a cassette player with Gloria Gaynor coming through the speakers singing "*I Will Survive*," and my mom sang right along with her. I asked my mom to please leave my room so I could continue to sit in my pain and cry about how my life was over, but she refused and told me to let that be the last time I ever cry over a guy. She gave me a few life lessons to help me through that difficult time, and it was a memorable mother-and-daughter moment that didn't mean much then, but it's one of my fondest memories now. That was still during a time I felt my mom didn't love me the way I thought a mother should; however, this is more evidence that she did show me love and care in her own way. I didn't see it then, but I see it now.

What were your first lessons about love that you can remember, and that shaped the way you view love?

_____

_____

_____

_____

_____

_____

_____

The relationships we form as a child and through our adult years say a lot about how we view ourselves and what type of bonds we are wanting to create. When I was younger, I tended to be friends with people who had mothers who made me feel loved and special in their homes. Some of those mothers let me call them Mom or Ma, and I would imagine them as my real mom. They would hug me, cook for me, invite me to family functions with them, and ask about my life. This actually fueled the anger I started to form with my mom and created more distance between us. Why couldn't she be concerned with what was going on in my life? Why wouldn't she hug me, or show me any type of affection? Whatever I felt I was lacking from my family, I looked for it in other families. This was also true with the boyfriends I had. The relationships I had with them lasted longer if I was close to their mom. It's wild what we discover about our past behaviors when we FINALLY go through healing and major self-awareness. More on that coming up.

When I think back on the relationships that didn't last with friends and even family members, most of those relationships ended or took a turn during the time I started healing. The journey into my healing began with several pieces working together. I needed to talk with someone who I felt would not judge me, who I could open up to without shame, and who could help me start to put my life in order. So, I started going to therapy around the time my daughter was four years old, and I didn't tell many people. Come to think of it, I'm not sure I told anyone at first, because I was fearful of my friends and family judging me. Therapy wasn't something I saw many people I knew do. Therapy was great for me, because I felt someone was truly hearing me, and not just telling me what they thought I wanted to hear or giving me advice based on their own beliefs that didn't always work for me. Having a therapist was a gateway for me to seek out other ways to heal.

I started journaling again, which was something I did almost daily as a child. Journaling was an outlet for me that I swear was its own version of healing. Whenever I put pen to paper, so many thoughts and emotions would come up for me that I didn't know were hiding just beneath the surface—and some thoughts were buried so deep I needed a spiritual shovel to dig them out. I was able to read what just came out of my mind and look at it from a totally new perspective. Journaling is something to this day that I do, because my journey is ongoing, so some of the practices that helped me then still help me now.

Another piece to my healing was switching jobs. I started working for a restaurant, and I loved so many things about it, especially the people who also worked there. It became my second job, because I was living paycheck to paycheck with my full-time job and I couldn't keep being that person who was always late paying bills. I made new friends with some of my co-workers at my new job, and I began to feel good in those relationships. I moved up quickly at the restaurant and went from being a server to a trainer then onwards to a traveling trainer. I was great at my job! I loved what I did there and I felt valued and respected, because I was learning how to value and respect myself through all of my new healing practices and fresh perspectives on my life. Other people valuing me doesn't mean much if I'm not valuing myself. Eventually, I quit my full-time job and began solely working for the restaurant. This was a blessing, because my 9 a.m.–6 p.m. job was draining me in many ways. The years at the restaurant were absolutely amazing; however, a few years later, the restaurant started to slow down, and I wasn't making as much money as I was before. I didn't want to leave, because I loved being there and the people I worked with. The reality was, I had to make more money in order for my daughter and me to survive. I decided to start working at a second restaurant and started teaching violin lessons again. Guess what? That still wasn't enough, so I started working for a company as an independent consultant on top of the other jobs I had. The company I joined was a game changer for me. Just like with the restaurant, I moved up quickly, and felt valued and appreciated. I was recognized for many areas for several years in a row, and had a lot of life changing moments during my time there. It became a huge part of my life, and it got to a point where I had to let the other jobs go, which I did within the first few years of being with this company. Leaving my main restaurant was difficult, but I knew it was time to move on. Also, just like at the restaurant, I made new friends at the company I was an independent consultant for and some of those friends became my chosen family.

Some of my friendships inside and outside of the ones I made at work changed as I started to see people for who they really were, how they made me feel, and how I felt around them. I was truly starting to like myself, which gave me the courage and strength to say goodbye to friendships that I held onto for years and become open to the type of friendships I wanted to create with people who I could grow with and who I believed I could trust. I deserved better relationships, and I was finally beginning to believe that.

My spirituality also started to become clearer to me and stronger. I was raised in a Pentecostal church, and I was led to believe that the only way to get closer to God was to live and breathe that religion, and that believing anything else would condemn me to an afterlife in hell. So, when I started to learn about other religions and spiritual practices, I felt guilt, shame, and fear; however, I wanted to discover God in a way that felt true to me. So, I set out on a path that felt right to me. I began to spend more time in nature. I learned how to trust in my spiritual gifts and began to meditate daily and most times throughout the day. (FYI, meditation isn't just sitting upright with crossed legs, eyes closed, with finger and thumb touching.) Faith, peace, and being present took on a whole new meaning for me, and I started to feel myself becoming whole.

I began a relationship with someone who was so different from other men I had dated. Guess what? I asked for him when I was a child. No joke! I remember the evening I went outside and had a heart-to-heart with God about him. I looked up in the sky and asked God to send me a life mate when I became an adult who was kind to others and to me, who was patient, would have fun with me, who would love me and cherish me, who would support my dreams, who would give me hugs whenever I needed them, who was not afraid to show his emotions, who was intelligent, who would cook for me (because cooking is not and has never been something I truly enjoy), and who would look at me with tenderness. Tim is all of that and then some! It was like I placed an order, and boom there he was... over fifteen years after my order was placed. He came into my life during the very early stages of my healing, when I was still making a lot of poor choices but learning and growing from them. As I became better for myself, our relationship grew stronger and we became closer. It's pretty challenging to have a healthy relationship with anyone—a friend, significant other, family member—if you are not right within yourself.

Another part of my healing journey was working on my physical health. Working out became a healthy release, and no, I'm not talking about working out to shed pounds. I used to work out excessively and weigh myself constantly, and that was so harmful to my health. While healing I started to view my physical body as the shell that's helping me move throughout my life. My weight and the scale were no longer my focus. My focus grew more on improving the chances of living longer and having a healthier life, and that meant getting my heart, liver, kidneys, blood, gut, limbs, and all other body parts in great shape! It meant doing what was necessary to decrease my chances of illnesses and diseases that could come from poor health. Eating foods that agree with my body and working out make me feel better overall, and I've completely eliminated my obsession with my weight. "Your weight and body size are the least interesting things about you." I first heard this quote from my friend Megan, and it has stuck with me because to me it's the truth! When I tell you this was a huge part of my healing, that is not an understatement.

So, you see my healing journey didn't just consist of one thing, it consisted of many things, and these are just some of the main parts that helped the most. This isn't even everything I did to heal, grow, and fall in love with myself. I also hired a personal development team, which consisted of a spiritual guide, a life coach, and a few other support systems. Was it easy? What do you think? HECK NO, it wasn't easy! Was it worth it? I'm alive, aren't I? So, I will say DARN SKIPPY it was worth it! In order to truly get better, I had to make changes in every single area of my life. That may not be the case for you, but this may be that sign you've been searching for (or hiding from, and you know what I'm talking about) that it's time for some sort of change in your own life.

What change(s) are necessary for you to grow, heal, and love yourself more?

_____

_____

_____

_____

_____

_____

What decision(s) have you been avoiding that you know may help you have more peace, joy, and love in your life?

_____

_____

_____

_____

_____

_____

_____

_____

What has not making these changes and decisions already cost you?

_____

_____

_____

_____

_____

_____

_____

_____

Not being healed, holding on to pain, being unforgiving, blaming everyone else for the direction of my life, and not respecting and valuing myself cost me:

* Time.

* Energy.

* Being in relationships that I didn't need to be in.

* Not being respected by others, because I wasn't respecting myself.

* Extremely unhealthy habits, which caused harm to my body.

* Emotional exhaustion.

* Feeling sad, angry, and confused.

* Feeling like I didn't have a purpose to live.

When a woman truly loves herself, she:

* Doesn't allow others to make her feel bad about herself, because she is confident in who she is.

* Will spend her time and energy with people who also love themselves and who are uplifting and positive.

* Views her overall health in HEALTHY ways, and this applies to mental health, spiritual health, emotional health, and physical health.

* Will not sacrifice her well-being for the sake of others, because she values herself.

* Knows without a doubt that she is worthy of living an incredible life and does whatever it takes to live that type of life.

* Encourages and uplifts others.

* Does not feel the need or desire to compare herself to others.

* Takes responsibility for her actions.

* Goes after her dreams and goals, regardless if others believe in her or not.

* Is a boundary setting QUEEN, and recognizes boundaries are loving and necessary for her overall health and the growth of the relationships she wants to nurture.

* Understands the power of forgiveness, and how it frees herself from hurt, trauma, and discomfort. Forgiveness is the key out of your own prison.

* Loves herself so gosh darn hard, that everyone else's love is a sweet bonus!

Self-love includes self-worth, self-validation, self-confidence, self-image, and self-satisfaction. It also includes a TON of self-awareness. When you are thriving in all of those areas, then you have become a woman who seriously loves herself!

This is not to say that women who love themselves don't have moments of doubt or feelings of insecurities. This means that women who love themselves have worked on getting to know themselves on deeper levels, recognizing what lifts them up and what brings them down, and have gained tools for their Self-Love Toolbox to help them through challenging times. Remember, towards the beginning of this book I talked a bit about the Self-Love Toolbox, and how throughout our lives, we will add tools as needed. We will continue to discover new ways to love ourselves, have gratitude for our lives, and appreciate the journey we have been on so far. However, the choice is yours if that is how you want to continue your life. We are all in the same boat, in which we have this one life to live here on earth. You may not be able to control everything that happens in your life; however, you are able to control how you respond, show up, and move through your life.

Taking control and responsibility of my own actions was something I had to do if I wanted to live better and feel better. And then something happened that changed my life forever, and that's when the deeper transformation took place.

The night of January 27, 2017, my mother, my youngest brother Chaun, and I were called to the hospital because my other brother, Darius, was in a car accident. We weren't told about his condition or what to expect. Each of us drove there hoping he only had a few minor injuries. When all three of us arrived, we were told that he was involved in a multiple-car accident and that he was the only fatality. My world stopped spinning. I thought I was having a mental breakdown. Nothing seemed real around me. "What do you mean he's gone?" I have never felt pain like that before. The grief took over my body. I seriously couldn't see straight or think clearly. "Wait, I can't see him?" I was losing my mind, and now I understood what real heartbreak felt like. There was no comforting me. There was no calming me down. Looking back I thought a piece of me died with him, but after a year had passed that was when I started to see everything in a completely new way.

Up until Darius passed away, I was doing much better in my life. I was liking myself more and feeling good about the direction of my life. I told you about all of the healing methods I had been doing, and they were working. But his death changed me, and eventually it changed me for the better—but not right away. The change first started when I realized I was a zombie on autopilot, with a blurred sense of reality. This went on for almost a year after he passed. Therapy was helping some, staying busy with work was helping a bit, the support of Tim and my friends was comforting, but I was not OK. I wasn't slipping back into my past thoughts and behaviors, but it was almost as if I was at a standstill and I didn't know what to do. The same year Darius passed away, Dona-Car'n graduated from high school, and Tim and I moved to Florida. There were so many big changes happening so close together, and I felt like there was so much noise in my head. I felt unsettled and unclear and I didn't like it. When we moved, Tim got a job right away and my business had slowed down a lot from being in a completely new area. My daughter decided to stay in Illinois, and our dogs were with my in-laws until we got settled in Florida. So, for the first time ever, I only had to focus on me.

I would go to the beach almost every day, and allow the power of being near and in the water give me a new level of peace. I spent a lot of time in silence indoors and outdoors. I stopped planning every minute of my life, and learned how to have more flow. I created healthy morning and bedtime routines, which were a big part in starting my days with joy and gratitude and ending them with contentment and gratitude. I continued to journal and meditate daily. I took myself out on dates, found new hobbies, read a lot of books, and, most importantly, I got to know myself in ways I never had before. I spent a lot of time reflecting on my past and being thankful for my growth. I grieved the way my role as a mother was changing now that my daughter was becoming a woman, and I wasn't expecting to grieve in that way. I grieved the loss of Darius, and I found ways to honor his life. I also grieved my past, which I didn't realize for so long was preventing me from fully moving forward. Grieving allowed me to feel free and light. This is when I started to truly forgive.

FORGIVENESS HELPED ME TO FEEL FREE

For over a year after Darius passed, I had nightmares almost nightly about him dying over and over again. Once I forgave the person who caused the accident my nightmares stopped. Now the dreams I have of Darius are sweet and gentle. My anger towards this person turned to compassion. No, I didn't have to go to this person to let them know I forgave them. This was about being free from the trauma and pain NOT forgiving him was causing me. I had to set my own self free, so I did.

For almost two decades I held on to the trauma caused by my abuser, and my thoughts were laced with fear and hatred. Once I forgave him, I no longer had bad thoughts about him. Just like with the person who caused the accident my brother was a part of, I did not tell my abuser personally that I forgave him. Initially the thought of forgiving him seemed absurd and I had no plans to forgive him, because I didn't feel he deserved my forgiveness. However, it wasn't about him. This was about freeing myself from what happened to me from his actions. This was also about not letting anyone, and I mean any and every living soul, have that much power over how I show up for myself. The person who caused me mental, emotional, and physical abuse is no longer someone I give my energy to. In the past when I would see him, I could feel my heart race, my blood pressure would go up, and I would have unkind thoughts about him. Now if I see him, there is no physical, mental, or emotional reaction. There is only peace. I love myself too much to let anyone disrupt the peace I now have in my life.

For most of my life I blamed my mother for almost everything that went wrong in my life. I blamed her for not loving me enough. I blamed her for not protecting me. I blamed her for the divorce between her and my father. I blamed her for whatever I thought she needed to be blamed for. That cost us years of not getting to truly know each other, and I would tell myself I didn't care if she was in my life, but I did care. I wanted my mom to see me, understand me, take interest in my life, protect me, and love me. Once I forgave her it felt like a weight the size of ten fully-grown elephants was lifted off of me. Here's the best part, we finally started to get to know each other as individuals first and then we started working on building up our mother and daughter relationship. This took creating boundaries for one another that we both had to respect, putting my ego to the side, time and patience on both sides, and coming to an understanding that we are accepting each other as we are and choosing to love each other as we are. For so long I wanted to change who she was and had certain expectations of her as my mother, but when we started to work on our relationship, I knew I wanted to get to know her as Donna, and then as my mom. Do we still have difficult moments with each other? I am happy to say we have reached a level where we can talk and work through any moment that isn't comfortable or agreeable with one or both of us. Before, it would be us avoiding each other, complaining about each other without coming up with a solution, and not even trying to listen to what the other person was saying or asking. We are past that. We ask each other questions now. We understand we show love to each other in different ways, and that's OK now. The difference with me forgiving my mother, and me forgiving the other guys, is that I did personally let her know how I felt because I want her in my life. There are many levels, degrees, and types of forgiveness. Forgiveness helped me heal, and now my mother and I say, "I love you," to one another. That is something we never did when I was growing up, or even in my twenties and early- to mid-thirties. The power of forgiveness is life changing.

If you're asking how I was able to forgive the person who caused the accident that led to my brother's death, the person who tormented me for years, and my mother who I felt didn't love or protect me, my answer is this... I first had to forgive myself. This was not an overnight process. Forgiving myself started all the way back when I first decided to commit to rediscovering myself and healing. Forgiving myself was when I decided to live my life on purpose and with love for myself.

During one of the stages of my personal transformation after moving to Florida, I asked myself how I could honor Darius' life, and I could hear his voice as clear as if he were sitting right by me, and he said, "Sister, stop wasting time." At that moment I knew what I had to do. I had to stop allowing whatever doubts and fears that were still lingering that I couldn't live 100 percent the way I wanted to live full out, and take action. I went into deeper awareness within to figure out what else was holding me back. I had made so much progress already, but there was still room for growth. There was still pain, resentment, fear, and doubt that kept visiting me, and it was time to kick those visitors out for good. I decided to truly LIVE and only do what felt good to me, up my gratitude meter, forgive and be forgiven, love and be loved, embrace my vulnerability, and take charge of my SELFIES!

Since my transformation and owning my self-worth, embracing self-validation, increasing my self-confidence, redefining what my self-image means to me, committing to self-satisfaction, and going from self-hate to majorly loving myself, many changes have happened in my life:

I spend more time with myself in silence, and feel more at ease in my life instead of in chaos or anxiousness.

I feel more connected to my spirituality than I ever have before, and this is because there is no guilt or shame around it. I am also owning and utilizing my spiritual gifts!

I take myself on dates whenever I feel like it, and those dates may cost money or may be free, but either way, they are priceless because they help me to continue loving and learning myself.

I am proud to call myself a Boundary Creating Queen! My mental health loves me for this!

I fully trust my intuition to make the right decisions for me.

I own the fact that I am a Magical Manifester! Don't you remember how as a child I journaled about what I would one day be doing to help women and turn it into a business?! I also told God what I wanted in a life partner (before I was even in seventh grade), and he delivered with bonuses in the form of my husband, Tim. Everyday I'm manifesting! Side note: manifestation isn't just asking for what you want and expecting it to just fall in your lap without doing anything. There's a formula to it! That's an entirely different book. Wink wink!

My relationship with my daughter, Dona-Car'n, is growing in love. We communicate in healthier ways, which was a challenge for us before. We are open and honest with each other, and we have lots of fun together. I also want to mention here that these are my daughter's top three favorite parts for our relationship, and I agree with her.

My relationship with my husband and life partner, Tim, has grown leaps and bounds and become stronger; we are more connected in all ways possible; and we truly support and encourage one another. Also, we have way more fun now that I'm a happier and more peaceful person.

You already know the deal with my mom and me. Our relationship has taken a 180-degree turn around. I look forward to our visits, and our phone calls. We are different people and we accept that and have learned to appreciate that about each other.

I have healthy friendships with people I enjoy spending time with, have deep conversations with, can be silly and totally myself with, have fun with (have you noticed I love to have fun!), and these friends love themselves and work towards creating better lives.

I went back to school and earned my degree, which took putting my ego to the side, kicking self-doubt to the curb, and not giving energy to what other people thought.

I cast fear and doubt to the side and decided to bring my childhood dream to life, and hosted my first R.A.W. retreat, which led to the start of my business.

I quit ALL of my jobs working for other people and other companies, and I am the owner and founder of Redesign and Align from Within, LLC.

I host transformational retreats in the U.S. and internationally to help women on their self-discovery journey.

I became a transformational mindset coach to help successful entrepreneur/career women learn how to put themselves first without the guilt, how to love themselves on all levels, and how to bring their wildest, most creative, and non-negotiable dreams to life.

Aaaaaaaaaaannnnnnddddddd, I wrote and published a book. You're reading it now! HEHEHE!

Most importantly I have healed past traumas and emotional wounds, and have the tools to continue healing in areas that need it.

There are so many ways my life has changed, but I kept the list short because this book doesn't need to be a thousand pages long. You read about my journey, and you read about ten other women in this book and their journeys. You have eleven examples of women who decided to take back their life, especially when they were in their darkest or most challenging times in their lives. These were stories where women were being their most vulnerable selves for the world to read to remind you that you are not alone. We are in this life together! I don't know every person who will read this book; however, what I do know is that each of us have so much within us that wants to be set free to get the most out of this life. It's time out for wasting any more of your energy, your time, or the well-being of your health on not living and loving your life fully.

Remember the woman I mentioned in the very beginning of this book who told me on our first coaching call together that she didn't know how to love herself? Well, she is no longer singing that same song. She is singing a new tune of I LOVE ME, and she has completely turned her life around. It started with being tired of not being completely satisfied with her life, and always being critical of how she looked, dressed, and appeared in front of people. She stopped saying she wanted to change and started showing herself and others that she was willing to do the inner work. Her closest relationships became stronger, she said goodbye to a friend who was draining her energy, her business revenue increased by 60 percent within a year, and she started dating someone who she feels comfortable with and has fun creating special moments with. She stopped being the "mean girl" to herself and turned into the cheerleader for herself. She took responsibility for her life, and now she is living in a way that brings a smile to her face.

It's time for you to take responsibility for how you show up for yourself and others.

It's time to get Redesigned and Aligned from Within!

It's time to love on your SELFIES with no "filters," no regret and with all of the possibility of your love going viral to the next level! It's time for YOU!

SELFIE TIME!

It's time for you to write a love letter to yourself. Please do not skip this part. This is for every person reading this book who has made it to the very end. This is your time to show yourself some love, take the "filters" off, and get raw and honest. This love letter can be to your past self, your current self, your future self, or a combination of the three.

Before you begin, take a moment to imagine I'm wrapping my arms around you, allowing you to lean into me as my breathing syncs up with yours, and you finally let all of your fears, worries, anxious thoughts, and shame leave you. No one can hurt you. No one can judge you. No one can love you the way you are able to love yourself. Do this for you, and no one else.

A LOVING R.A.W MESSAGE FROM ME TO YOU:

You are not lost. You are not broken. You are not unlovable. Claim what you are! Claim who you are! Speak love, joy, peace, and fun into your life and take any step towards receiving it. A small step is a step. An unsure step is a step. A shaky step is a step. Just take the dang blasted step! You are so gosh darn worthy of having the life you want to create. You are worth being forgiven and being able to forgive. You are worth having fun in your life. You are worth LIVING your life, and not just going through the motions. You are worth bringing any of your dreams and goals to life. You are worthy of seeing yourself for who you truly are, and not based on who or what you see in the mirror. You are here for a reason. You read this book for a reason. Those feelings that have stirred up inside of you from reading this book and doing (or avoiding) the activities are trying to send you a message. Now is the time to pay attention to what you want and need most. You have one known life on this earth, how are you choosing to live it?

THE LADIES AND I WANTED TO CREATE AND SHARE A PLAYLIST OF SONGS THAT HELPED US ALONG OUR SELF-DISCOVERY JOURNEY. ENJOY!

ASHLEY

"This is Me" from The Greatest Showman Soundtrack

In a big world of unknowns, learning to trust your own intuition can be difficult to navigate, especially when you are used to doing things to receive praise from others. This song was my battle cry. It was my strength anthem on many days to show up. This is me, the good, the bad, the ugly. This is what I have to offer—change that—what I want to offer and with that I am perfectly content.

BRITTANY

"Fight Song" by Rachel Platten

This song reminds me to keep fighting to be the person I know I am deep down inside, even on the days I hear that little voice that's telling me, "I'm not good enough!"

This song also empowers me to keep living a life that's authentic to me and to never forget that I have the power within me to keep living life on my own terms!

It is my hope that when you listen to this song you believe in yourself even if no one else does. Remember that you are worthy to keep "fighting" for the person you know you are, and for the life you know you deserve!

JAIMIE

"(I'm Gonna) Love Me Again" by Elton John

When I first heard this song, I couldn't stop smiling. It gave me so much life! It is a reminder that we are ALL worthy of putting ourselves first. That we should all start LOVING ourselves, no matter what the circumstance.

KATRINA

"Rise" by Lost Frequencies

This song is a reminder to pick yourself back up after a hard time. To keep fighting, to keep rising, to keep believing in yourself. When you listen to it, I hope you'll feel the inspiration to keep elevating.

KAYLA

"Miss Me More" by Kelsea Ballerini

"Miss Me More," chose me. When I heard it, I was in a space in my life where I really had lost myself in a relationship, and I realized what I missed most... Was me.

NAKRISTIN

"Lose to Win" by Fantasia Barrino

The song reminded me that even if I lose, I'll still win. Every time I listened to it, I digested the lyrics and applied it to my life and how I was feeling. Even if I lost a lot, I won more because I had overcome so many things, and even if I didn't feel like I was winning, I knew that if I kept repeating, "Sometimes you gotta lose to win again," I would believe it more and more. Through any situation, whether it's a job loss or losing someone, I looked for the positives in every situation because the loss could have been so much worse.

RUTH

"Symphony" by Switch

This song wrapped up how I was feeling in a bow, and reminded me that God was working on a bigger plan in my life behind the scenes. I just needed to trust in him and be patient.

SHANNA

"Survivor" by Destiny's Child

This song reminds me every day that even though I went through what I did it made me a stronger survivor, mother, and person. The past didn't determine or hinder my current and future life. It just made it better. I decided to surround myself with positive things and positive people. I'm stronger than I have ever been, all because of what I had to go through to get to the woman I am today. You can get to this point; you just have to believe in yourself and your capability to walk away from someone or something that no longer serves you. You are strong. You are beautiful. Most importantly, YOU are WORTHY!

STACEY

"Praying" by Kesha

"Praying" made me realize that I am worth so much more that I thought and that I wish no ill will on anyone in my past but hope that they are at peace in their lives now.

NINA

You Are a Badass by Jen Sincero

In times I didn't believe in myself, I had this Audible book in my corner filling my cup until I believed in all that she was saying!

DENISE

"Ain't No Mountain High Enough" by Marvin Gaye
and Tammi Terrell

This song is a reminder that nothing will stand in my way of giving myself the life and love I deserve. I love, appreciate, and respect myself enough to give myself what I need and desire most. My wish is that when you listen to this song you may feel the same way. This is your one known life on this earth... You deserve to live it in a way that feels OH SOOO GOOD!

ACKNOWLEDGEMENTS

To the women who were brave enough to share their stories in this book, THANK YOU! Each of you knew that letting others take a peek into your journey would help so many people in myriad ways. This was an act of love for yourself and others, owning your vulnerability, and moving past your fears. I respect each of you, I appreciate each of you and I truly love each one of you. Ashley, Brittany, Jaimie, Katrina, Kayla, NaKristin, Nina, Ruth, Shanna and Stacey.

To my daughter, Dona-Car'n, you gave me the courage and permission to write this book. There were so many parts of me that I wasn't sure if I wanted to share with others, and you encouraged me and told me to do it anyway if it would help at least one person. You remind me daily that we are not our past shame, trauma, or experiences. We have the choice and the chance to grow from what we've gone through, learn from those who have loved and hurt us, and create new experiences that we are proud of and thankful for. I am proud of you, and thankful that I was chosen to be your mom. I love you, Tink!

To my husband, Tim—You are the one who chooses every day to walk beside me in this life, and you continue to be the man I choose to walk with in this world that is full of so many unknowns. You have loved me, encouraged me, appreciated me, taught me, and have grown with me for over fifteen years. Our pasts led us to each other to live out the rest of our future together, and I am grateful for that. Thank you for holding my hand in the most difficult times, and in the most joyous times. Thank you for hugging me every time I needed it. Most importantly, I thank you for never trying to change me. I love you, babe!

To my mom—I always knew you would be a part of my first book, and I didn't know until I started writing this book how much of this book is because of you. You told me that you raised me to be resilient, and I must say you did a great job! I am resilient, because of you. I am able to face difficult challenges head on, because of you. I am able to stand firm in my beliefs, my will, and my abilities, because of you. I spent so many years not acknowledging how much you have taught me, shown me, or loved me, and I cannot thank God enough for giving me the opportunity to acknowledge who you are to me and what you mean to me now. Thank you for raising me to be independent, resourceful, and brave, just like you! I love you, Mother!

To my brothers, Darius and Chaun—I have gone through a repeated cycle of emotions thinking about how you both are no longer physically here on this earth. I know without a doubt that you both would be celebrating with me BIG TIME right now, and encouraging me in ways that only a brother could. There were moments during writing this book that felt extremely hard, and I didn't know if this book would ever be completed. In those moments I would feel the presence of both of you. I would imagine you both standing next to me telling me to not give up, and remember why I'm doing this. To say I miss you both is an understatement. Thank you, Darius, for reminding me to not give up on what I want, and thank you for being the voice that started this R.A.W. journey for me. Thank you, Chaun, for reminding me that I am fully supported and loved, especially during the times I need it most.

To the Get It Done Team—I appreciate all of your encouragement, support, and guidance. Going through this experience with the entire team has made the tough days seem not so tough, and made the exciting stages even more exciting. I appreciate each of you for cheering me on, and being an important part of this experience! Now, it's time for book two!

ADDITIONAL RESOURCES

National Suicide Prevention Lifeline: 800-273-8255

National Domestic Violence Hotline: 800-799-7233

Alcoholics Anonymous: aa.org

Narcotics Anonymous: na.org

If you are experiencing depression, anxiety, postpartum, or a miscarriage, I want to encourage you to seek support immediately. You do not have to go through this alone. The women in this book and I understand the pain and loneliness these challenges may cause. We see you!

BIBLIOGRAPHY

Harvard University Center on the Developing Child. "Serve and Return." Accessed July, 2022. https://developingchild.harvard.edu/science/key-concepts/serve-and-return/.

Simpson, Alison. 2021. "Majority of women struggle with self-esteem issues." *Current Affairs for Women, Featuring on WATC, International Women's Day News*, March 8, 2021. URL.

American Psychological Association: APA Dictionary of Psychology. "Self-worth." Accessed July 2022. https://dictionary.apa.org/self-worth.

Aubrey, Allison. 2008. "Happiness: It Really Is Contagious." *npr*, December 5, 2008. https://www.npr.org/2008/12/05/97831171/happiness-it-really-is-contagious.

Merriam Webster Dictionary. "Self-confidence." Accessed July, 2022. https://www.merriam-webster.com/dictionary/self-confidence.

Hall, Karyn. "Self-Validation." Pieces of Mind (blog). Psychology Today. July 12, 2014. https://www.psychologytoday.com/us/blog/pieces-mind/201407/self-validation

The Counseling Center at University of South Florida, A Department of Success, Top Concerns. *"What is Self-Confidence?."* Accessed July, 2022. https://www.usf.edu/student-affairs/counseling-center/top-concerns/what-is-self-confidence

Hogan, Matt. *"Choose Your Hard."* Beyond the Quote (blog). Move Me Quotes. December 5, 2020. https://movemequotes.com/choose-your-hard/.

Merriam Webster Dictionary. "Self-image." Accessed July, 2022. https://www.merriam-webster.com/dictionary/self-image.

Cleveland Clinic Health Library. "Fostering a Positive Self-Image." Accessed July, 2022. https://my.clevelandclinic.org/health/articles/12942-fostering-a-positive-self-image.

Ackerman, Courtney. "Life Satisfaction Theory and 4 Contributing Factors." Happiness & SWB (blog). PositivePsychology.com. November 6, 2018. https://positivepsychology.com/life-satisfaction/

Ackerman, Courtney. "Life Satisfaction Theory and 4 Contributing Factors." Happiness & SWB (blog). PositivePsychology.com. November 6, 2018. https://positivepsychology.com/life-satisfaction/.

Dhanashree. "Self Satisfaction: A Key to Success." Stay Ahead (blog). Bannari Amman Institute of Technology. August 10, 2020. https://blog.bitsathy.ac.in/self-satisfaction-a-key-to-success/

Love Songs: The Hidden History. 2016. Video. https://www.loc.gov/item/webcast-7427/.

AUTHOR BIO

Denise Marsh is the author of *Do It For Your SELFIE!: A Guide to Loving Yourself, Redesigning Your Life, and Getting Aligned from Within,* and founder of R.A.W.: Redesign & Align from Within, LLC. As a Transformational Mindset Coach and speaker, Denise works with women to increase their self-love and self-awareness so they can feel more confident in making their dreams and desires a priority. She mentors with passion, guiding her clients to effectively strengthen and elevate their mindset to new heights.

Denise engages individuals and groups during her transformational services, including customized coaching, retreats, her podcast, as well as through other platforms and leaves them with empowering tools and focused mindsets that they will use long after their experience with her. Denise is passionate about people, living life full out and making a difference wherever she goes. She is especially inspired to help people take their dreams – and themselves – to levels they didn't believe was possible.

When not speaking, hosting a retreat or working with clients, Denise can be found traveling with her husband, connecting with her only daughter and grandson, snuggling with her fur babies with a mug of hot tea, having a random solo dance party, or reading a good book at the beach.

Learn more at: DeniseMarsh.net or
https://linktr.ee/denisemarshraw